Pathways to Personal Freedom using the Silva Method

DIANA SILVA & ROBERT DEUTCHMAN

BALBOA.
PRESS
A DIVISION OF HAY HOUSE

Balboa Press books may be ordered through booksellers or by contacting:

Balboa Press
A Division of Hay House
1663 Liberty Drive
Bloomington, IN 47403
www.balboapress.com
1 (877) 407-4847

Print information available on the last page.

ISBN: 978-1-9822-2060-0 (sc)
ISBN: 978-1-9822-2062-4 (hc)
ISBN: 978-1-9822-2061-7 (e)

Library of Congress Control Number: 2019900877

Balboa Press rev. date: 05/22/2019

Dedicated to the memories of Jose Silva Sr. and Dr. Wayne W. Dyer—

Spiritual beings who changed humanity with their wisdom, insight, foresight, and God-given abilities and set the pathways for a better world.

Forever in our hearts ...

Special thank you to Yasemin Yavaslar, Silva graduate of the Silva Method for Mind Control, for her wonderful editing, professionalism, and unwavering support to help bring our vision to fruition. May you continue to always radiate love and light to your loved ones and to all who are blessed to come across your path.

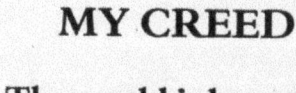

MY CREED

**The world is beautiful
The people are great
Everything is wonderful
I am glad I am here and alive!**

Marty Sloane
1973

ABOUT THE AUTHORS

Diana Silva, daughter of Jose Silva, the creator of Silva Mind Control, has dedicated her life to helping others. She is the president of Silva International and has more than thirty years of experience supporting Silva Graduates and the International Community of Silva Instructors. She has helped people around the world using the Silva Method Mental Techniques with state-of-the-art coaching methodologies to bring her clients to a more advanced state of living.

Diana helps people find their true loves, soul mates, and happiness in life by learning to love others and themselves with balance and boundaries. She also helps others looking for new jobs or career paths to align with the purpose of their lives. She helps people understand the spiritual-based steps that begin in the real world. She possesses degrees in counseling and theology. She lives in Laredo, Texas, with her husband, Ruben Mendez, and son, Nikolas Ruben Mendez.

Robert Deutchman is a senior recreation therapist and group coordinator for the Office of Mental Health in New York State. He utilizes recreation therapy combined with music to enhance the lives of others in need of psychiatric care and community placement.

A student of modern-day spiritualists, Robert studied the teachings of Dr. Wayne W. Dyer, Deepak Chopra, and Louise Hay. He has many years of experience working with the elderly, short-term rehabilitation, and substance abuse populations utilizing meditation and visualization with his clients. He possesses a bachelor's degree in recreation administration from Kean University in Union, New Jersey. He lives in Staten Island, New York, with his wife, Wendy, and children, Arielle and David.

FOREWORD

My dad, Dr. Wayne W. Dyer, was a great teacher of self-reliance. His work has inspired millions around the world to look within for peace and happiness. In his later years, he taught that we were, in fact, all extensions of God and encouraged us to tap into the God Force within. He led by example and shared many personal accounts of his life and ours.

In addition to his many accomplishments, he was a graduate of The Silva Method, a self-help program that was instrumental in his own life. The Silva Method is a worldwide system that has helped millions achieve balance, serenity, and the ability to make life on this planet better and better. Dad used the visualization techniques created by Jose Silva Sr., which he wrote about in his book *Real Magic*, to cure himself of a hernia that he was told would require surgery.

Robert Deutchman is coauthor of the book you now hold. Along with Diana Silva, they created these Pathways and affirmations. Robert shared with me how my dad's books and teachings have impacted him, as well as the coincidences that led him to team up with Diana (the youngest daughter of Jose Silva Sr.). Their friendship evolved into this collaboration of Pathways you now hold.

Robert came across the Silva Method when his family was dealing with a personal crisis. His late uncle, who was a Silva Method graduate, taught him the techniques to jump-start recovery and wellness for a family member with severe depression. When Robert succumbed to his own depression years later, he rediscovered the course with the assistance of his chiropractor, Dr. Bruce Eisenberg. Later, the internet and social media connected Robert and Diana, and their vision encompassed an expansion of the Silva Method to be used for not only graduates and Silva enthusiasts but to all mankind.

My book, *Don't Die With Your Music Still In You,* is an account of my life growing up with spiritual parents and my interpretation of Dad's best-selling book, *10 Secrets to Success and Inner Peace.* I was taught very young that there is purpose to everything. Though I did not come to fully appreciate this realization until I was much older, I now know that the Universe is on purpose—always has been and always will be. When our minds are open and centered, we can align ourselves with Higher Intelligence, which will never lead us astray.

Read and enjoy these Pathways with an open heart and mind and allow the bliss of inner freedom to radiate from you, to the Universe, and back!

Serena Dyer

CONTENTS

INTRODUCTION

As you read the pages that follow, keep in mind that this book was written exclusively for you—the reader. Though we may not have formally met as of yet, we have something in common—a desire for a magnificent life, one that flows with inner peace combined with a sense of true freedom on this journey of life. With our own personal quest for enlightenment, joy, love, and prosperity, we're continuously reminded that these attributes are not merely something we find. Rather, they're something we indeed are, and we can learn to tune into them. The benevolence we are alluding to lies deep within our souls, and so many of us have yet to tap into this inner fortress.

This is not something we necessarily attain by making a single choice via positive thinking, though we certainly advocate it as a jump-start toward the betterment of the self and the world we share. Rather, this is an ongoing journey to be reinforced day after day, moment by moment.

Perhaps the invisible force that connects all things is what brought us together—to learn and grow. At the conclusion of your reading, we'd like to know how this book has impacted you. If enough feedback is received, we will write a follow-up book with your words to expand these ideas to better ourselves and to positively impact our world. Please understand that the intent is to help you—the reader—learn from us, and we can certainly learn from each other and share our thoughts and experiences.

When our minds and hearts are receptive to new ideas, the Universe conspires to bring whatever it is we want and need for inner peace and freedom. There really are no accidents, and a greater force connects all the so-called coincidences—all of them.

At this time, we are asking you to consider this: Anything and everything that has ever happened to you was supposed to. All the good, bad, and indifference was necessary on this path of life. You may be resistant to this at first. We're not asking you to pretend that anything hurtful should be overlooked and swept under the rug. We all have a personal history of trauma, guilt, shame, remorse, and the like. For now, just consider as you are reading these words that whatever it is we have encountered up until now, at the very least, cannot unhappen. With that realization in mind, we can, at least, suspend our skepticism and accept that everything up until now had a reason for happening.

When we step aside and analyze our lives from the perspective of today, we can look back with a quiet acceptance for everything—even if only briefly. There is a reason for all that *has* happened and all that *will* happen.

Like most, we get stuck in the it-is-not-fair and why-me traps. We all have lists of things we'd rather have done differently, as well as the so-called should-haves lists. Keep this in the forefront of your mind as you read on and see if you feel a shift in your thinking. You will come to know the truths as they emerge.

This book is divided into Pathways. Each Pathway has offerings for your benefit with the intention of bringing about your personal best and inner freedom. Whether you have been on this path for many years, are a Silva Method graduate, trainer, enthusiast, or an individual who has decided to take control from the inside out, we trust that our sharing will resonate within you a sense of inner harmony that will impact you and our world.

At the end of each Pathway, you'll find affirmations—positive statements usually pertaining to the present moment. The ideas are set in place to personally assist you with the contents and goals of each Pathway.

Thank you for allowing us to provide you with what we know will be a vast experience of joy, growth, and love. Please email us at Balboa Press and let us know your thoughts on our book.

Wishing you a joyous Pathway to your inner peace and freedom,

Diana Silva
Robert Deutchman

PATHWAY 1

Serenity as a Choice

The way we react to circumstances determines our feelings.

—Dale Carnegie

Have you ever noticed how relaxed and serene everyone gets when sitting in traffic? Neither have we! How about those waiting at the doctor's office for a half hour longer than expected? Or wishing your spouse would for once be ready to leave for the movies on time? You have probably experienced an array of events when your patience has been tested, such as the dreaded line at the local motor vehicle office. Who has not counted how many people are ahead by staring at the clock up front displaying the present number—which is far from the one assigned to you? "How much longer? Why do they always make us wait?" Endless thoughts keep you stuck in the present moment filled with stress, anxiety, boredom, and anger.

Being stuck is a label that is given when a very natural part of life occurs: not much is happening. Experiencing stillness makes most people anxious. But it is a golden opportunity to utilize your mind in creative ways to form ideas, plan the future, and think about what's right with your life.

Rearrange the Scene

Let us go back to the motor vehicle office. You show up fully prepared for the time between signing in and being called. You're equipped with your laptop, so you're writing down five things that you're grateful for, surfing the net, and reading an inspiring book on your electronic reader, giving you immediate peace. You might write a poem or compose lyrics to a hit song—the possibilities are endless. You are so caught up in your reverie that when your number is finally called, you ask for five more minutes—okay, that may be stretching it a bit, but you get the idea. You have made the time work *for* you instead of *against* you.

Perhaps you forgot your laptop or reader at home. Offices and waiting rooms are saturated with magazines and periodicals. If you enjoy reading, you have a way to rearrange the scene for your benefit. Or you can try something you may not have considered before.

Meditation and Affirmations

Truthfully, there is no right or wrong way to meditate. The Silva Method explains in detail how to achieve a level of mind for positivity and your benefit. While these techniques are scientifically proven and highly recommended by Silva Graduates worldwide, you are encouraged for the time being to just be still, breathe deeply, and implement the techniques in order to get the results desired. Know that mastery of any technique takes time and practice.

It's crucial to meditate daily to be in tune and aware of exactly what you want and don't want. By this, we mean being so connected with your mind, heart, and soul that you need no external stimulation to understand your inner desires. It means to know what you ache for—and to choose to discard what drains you.

Awareness does not come easy. Being aware and then making a start is equally difficult. Making a start and going all the way—that is *huge*!

When you learn to meditate and surrender to the stillness of your mind, you will discover new feelings of joy and delight. Beginning meditators can focus on quieting the mind by counting backward from ten to one, inhaling deeply, and exhaling on each number. This can be done with your eyes open or closed, depending on where you are, while counting down to yourself. There will be more on meditation later—but for now, just focus on breathing slowly, counting backward from ten to one.

Stating affirmations daily brings incredible power to everyday living. Affirmations should be repeated often. They are positive statements, usually for each now, that describe a desired goal until it gets impressed into your subconscious mind so that you can manifest it in the real world of life or at least guide you in the direction of your goal.

Even famous people use affirmations to enhance their performance. It is the repetition of affirmations that leads to belief. And once that belief becomes a deep belief of faith, positive things begin to happen.

For more on meditation, please see The Silva Centering Exercise at the end of the book.

Surrender

When we talk about the word *surrender,* we are in no way implying giving up. What we mean is to give in to the moment of true acceptance. If you stay completely peaceful in this moment, there is no being stuck—you realize it is just a label you invented based on a perception of the current time. When you become aware of this, breathe a deep sigh of relief. The feelings do not necessarily go away, but they no longer control you.

When you come to know that only you can control your feelings, you not only take on the delicious flavor of being at peace but take full credit for all that is serving you.

You will then see the play of thoughts. You might resist this act of surrendering. But with practice, you will get better and better at learning to let things be as they may. The occasional slip of being stuck will not hinder you. Rather, it will serve as a reminder that you must rearrange your thoughts about your circumstances, meditate, or do whatever you can to enjoy the moment now, which is really the only moment you can ever live.

Enjoy Your Life to the Fullest—Now!

Whatever it is that you enjoy, commit to doing at least one of those things today—or tomorrow if you are nearing bedtime. Why? Because it is something you enjoy, and you certainly deserve to treat yourself. You may feel guilty during this time. Your mind may be off and running with thoughts of things you should be doing instead of enjoying yourself. But past and future responsibilities will have to wait. This is your time. Allow yourself to enjoy it. If you have deadlines to meet, take just a half hour to do something totally for yourself. Stay in the moment, and if you slip back to thoughts of what you believe you should be doing, recognize it as a slip and know that anything new involves practice and persistence. Go easy on yourself.

Put It on Paper

Make a detailed list of what you enjoy. This is a very personal list—not one that anyone else can create. What brings you pleasure? Movies? Writing? Bowling? Running? Swimming? Museums? Just get started and watch your list grow. You will surprise yourself with all that is available to enjoy. I like to write by hand, the old-fashioned way. It seems to clear my mind more when I put it on paper than when I type it on my computer, but you do what works for you.

While you are at it, try writing without omitting any feelings. No looking back! Let everything flow. Make journaling your thoughts and feelings an everyday occurrence. Look for patterns and see if there is anything you would like to change or modify in your life. When you have done this for a few days, look back and view the ongoing events of your day objectively. You will know if you have lived life to the fullest and experienced joy and pleasure. The more you do this, the better you will see patterns of effective, present-moment living. When you truly become aware of what goes on inside you, you will come to know the folly of prior suffering and start living life to the fullest.

Quiet Acceptance

When we resist what is, we suffer. This holds true with everything in life. Learn to see resistance as an indicator to relax. Seeing that we can only do our best with what we have at the moment provides true inner peace and tranquility. Meditate with a clear mind to evaluate the steps to be taken with no force. Say to yourself: Life lives itself through me because I am life. I am not separate from anything or anyone because I am the moon, I am the stars, I am the sun, and I am you!

Sometimes we feel a lack of support or validation in life. Each person comes into this world through a womb, supported by his or her mother. The earth, microorganisms, and other trees support trees in the forest. Yet we believe we are alone. Are we? We get caught up in life and feel that things should be different than they are. But the fact is that life is not what you think it is.

Let Things Be

Whether you feel stuck for a day or a week, it does not really matter. You do the best you can with what you have. But the longer you are stuck, the longer you need to surrender.

Robert: The darkest periods of my life have taught me the most about myself. I have learned that life is not only about accomplishments. It is also about resting—surrendering and letting things be. Once you accept what is, your perception will actually change what is.

The decision can be made right at this moment—affirming that boredom is no longer a part of your life. Remember that you are too important to ever wallow in dull moments. Share this new way of being with those who encourage your growth. Otherwise, keep it to yourself, as there will always be those who will not buy into your quest for inner peace and tranquility—and they will try to dissuade you. Surround yourself with those who support you.

Affirmations

- Right now, I accept that I don't have all the answers to life's problems.
- I allow things to be as they are, rearrange circumstances when I get stuck, and never choose boredom.
- I share my new techniques only with those who support me on my path to peace and inner tranquility.

PATHWAY 2

Living a Happier Life

Live your belief and you can turn the world around.
—Henry David Thoreau

Diana: I found the man of my dreams, and as we chatted while dancing through the evening, we fell in love. To me, it seemed like heaven, though life had other plans. After that day, I never saw him again but continued to be in love with him. I felt consumed by the belief that he was my soul mate and that destiny someday would bring us back together again.

Isn't it strange how we all have our own beliefs about the secret to what makes us happy? We live our lives in agreement with those beliefs, and we hardly question them.

As time went by, my belief that I could never be happy with anyone else held me back from finding my true love and happiness in life. But I was so wrong. I met someone else and have been blessed with him for many years. We determine our realities by what we believe; therefore, our beliefs make us who we are and decide the choices we make. But oftentimes those beliefs bring us lots of pain and trouble.

Here are a few beliefs that make us unhappy.

I Need Outside Approval to Be Happy

Do you find yourself doing things only to keep other people happy? Human beings are driven by social approval. We buy the latest gadgets just to look good. We attend boring office gatherings just to fit in. We do not go after our dreams because our family members do not approve of them. But ask yourself if these actions or inactions bring you any real happiness. The search for approval is different from the pursuit of happiness. We need to learn how to distinguish between the two.

I Will Be Happy When I Have …

… A vacation house, a promotion, a new car, respect, and so on. Yes, you will *feel happy* when you get promoted or buy a vacation house. The question here is, will this happiness last?

Yes, you will do away with the dealings of your landlord. However, having a new house requires you to pay taxes and spend good money maintaining it. Each level of accomplishment will bring its own set of problems. Does this mean you stop working toward your goals? No, never stop! Goals are important, and one needs to be ambitious. Yet think about this: you can be happy *now* and when you get the promotion. Do you really need to postpone your happiness?

I Cannot Be Happy Unless Everything Goes Right

Have you ever lost your luggage when you went on a vacation? It upsets everything and everyone, doesn't it? Instead of enjoying a wonderful new city or country, you are running around buying clothes and other things that are needed, wondering if the airline will ever return your luggage. That is what happened on a vacation. Now, when we remember our trip, the issues we went through because of lost luggage no longer bother us. We just talk about the memorable time we had.

The vacation did not have to be perfect. The only thing that really mattered was the opportunity to have a great time together. Think about it: Are vacations, gatherings, dates, or any other special occasions *ever* perfect? If something goes wrong does that mean the entire trip or evening is a failure? It can be, but only if you *believe* it will be. But consider this: Is anything in life ever perfect? Everyone has ups and downs. Life is supposed to be imperfect because we are imperfect beings, and maybe that is what makes life more interesting.

Happiness Is Not Part of My Life because of My Past

For some reason, the past controls us in mysterious ways. You might have lost a loved one to a misunderstanding or death. You might have failed to achieve your dreams. Therefore, as a result, you may have developed one of these beliefs: I am not meant to find happiness, happiness is not who I am, it is not my destiny to be happy, and so on.

Diana: I myself have not lost much in life—thank God—but I know someone who has: my best friend. I used to wonder how she could enjoy life despite such tragedies until she gave me her secret. She believes that she has the *right* to be happy, despite her past mishaps.

Remember, your past does not control your future unless *you* allow it to. So just remind yourself that there are millions of people who have turned their lives around and so can you.

Happiness Is Not a Habit That Can Be Learned

Can one learn to be happy? Is it like learning to dance or playing the guitar? Of course it is. Happiness *is* a skill—one that you build through daily choices. It is said that people who are happier have positive habits because they exercise and meditate daily and pay attention to their relationships at work and at home. They go after their goals diligently, lead balanced lives, and are grateful for everything. It is believed that by preventing negative emotions, such as pessimism, resentment, and anger, and nurturing positive emotions, such as compassion, serenity, and gratitude, the brain can be trained to become happier. Happiness does not depend on fate; it depends on our habits, which anyone can learn.

Our beliefs can bring us happiness or sorrow. Therefore, it is good to question your beliefs about yourself, your life, and your happiness from time to time. That is the best way to see if they still serve a positive purpose for you. If they don't, change them fast.

Ask yourself what beliefs you think you need to change to be happier.

Affirmation

- I always think of myself in a positive light, and I make changes I believe will always make me happy.

PATHWAY 3

Clearing Your Mind of the Can't Mentality

If you think you can do a thing or you think
you can't do a thing, you're right.

—Henry Ford

Ways to Clear Your Mind of the Can't Mentality

We all have goals, ambitions, and dreams. Some of us persevere quite well, but others need a helping hand. Your mindset is the biggest difference between these two groups, and it varies from person to person as well as each desire. Sometimes your mindset is *can*; other times it is *can't*.

If you are currently experiencing difficulties in achieving what you want out of life, there is hope. You can clear your mind of those thoughts that are sabotaging your progress. Even if you are successful and happy, enhancing your natural abilities to motivate yourself and clearing mental roadblocks can bring you to a new level.

Realize You Are Holding Yourself Back

This can certainly be difficult to accept, but it holds true. Most of us are prideful and avoid accountability for ourselves at times. However, when you realize that only you have the control over your life, it is a tremendously powerful motivator.

Notice the word *realize*. It is there because many of us are not even aware of the fact that we are the major roadblock—not coworkers, bosses, or anyone else.

When it comes to rationalization, *making excuses*—the internalization of perceived failure— affects self-esteem, which negatively affects your thoughts and behavior. In other words, we are not good at letting go.

We must release our perceived failures in order to succeed in this lifetime. We can do that by being present in every situation, whether at work, home, any social setting, and especially when you are alone— the time your mind tends to go off and running. *Staying focused on what needs to be done in the present without rehashing past failures is the answer.*

Reverse the Can't to Can

This may sound repetitive, but we are the completeness of our thoughts. Therefore, it is important to affirm and declare your goals to help motivate your thinking, more so during the difficult times.

Some How-to Guides on Using Affirmations

- Identify and write down negative self-talk and beliefs or can'ts.
- Create and write down positive affirmations (cans), which are opposite of the first list.

- Begin using the new affirmations; place the written list in an area that you can see frequently to remind yourself.
- See miracles happen right before your eyes for your better good.

For example, change "I can't ever get what I want" to "I always strive for what I want." Change "I'm so awkward" to "I get better every day." Change "I'll never graduate" to "I will graduate." And change "I'll never be happy at work" to "I have many things to be grateful for."

Catch yourself whenever you make a can't statement and mentally reverse it to one that will serve you in a positive manner. Take notice of how often the people you encounter make a can't statement. While you may be tempted to share your new way of thinking with others, remember that this is *your* growth, and people do not like to be told how or what to think. The techniques here will be demonstrated by you, which will allow the right people to sense your growth and will make you more desirable to be around.

Remind Yourself of What You Have Overcome

It is normal to want to be more and achieve more. That is healthy. It is what keeps us going. With that being said, we need to remind ourselves of our past successes from time to time. This is important because when we feel stuck, past accomplishments serve as a reminder of the potential we each have inside of us to achieve success. It is a point of reference for you to lean on, especially when you need to be reminded of how powerful you are.

Your life was not handed to you on a plate; you had to earn it. Give yourself some credit for overcoming negative obstacles as they have presented themselves to you through life because you have become a stronger person having gone through these journeys. This overwhelming positive strength makes it possible for you to move forward and continue your path in life.

Accept That You Are Worthy

Do you accept who you are as a person? What features do you love about yourself? These are two questions that you will come to answer with a resounding *yes*. The truth is there is nothing wrong with you. Whatever shortcomings you believe you have will be overcome with time and effort, but they do not mean that you lack worth as a person.

Self-acceptance is a must in order to live a fulfilling life. You must let go of the thought patterns and behaviors that are in the way of growth. Often, it is a matter of perception. We can choose to perceive ourselves as unworthy and handicapped, or we can focus on our strengths and capabilities and reach for the stars.

Negative thoughts truly can be damaging. They are not the same as negative inner dialogue or self-talk. Self-talk is an actual voice inside your head. It is your inner voice. Thoughts are more elusive and difficult to pin down in terms of origin. Let them go or switch them to a positive affirmation. If you feel your behavior needs to be changed, then change it. But never believe you are unworthy to live a fulfilling, fruitful life and can be all that you desire.

When you accept yourself, you allow self-love to manifest. Self-love is simply the act of living while remaining true to yourself. It is an expression of your own acceptance, allowing you to support your progress through life. This is not applied only to your finances and career. Your emotional, psychological, and spiritual growth is where the self-love truly occurs.

Take Action

Many of us get caught up in thinking of everything at once to reach a goal. This leads to inactivity, procrastination, and avoidance. This lessens our motivation to accomplish the difficult but necessary tasks to achieve our goals.

The solution? Just take the first step. For example, you want to get into better shape. (Who doesn't?) Getting into better shape requires exercise and eating right. You know that going to the gym and changing your eating habits is all that is needed, but you resist.

Robert: First, put on your workout clothing. Then, just walk out the door. Now that you are out of the house, it would be kind of silly to walk back inside. You just jump-started the steps toward your goal of exercising. This may not seem like much, but this is a huge accomplishment for not wanting to go to the gym in the first place. I cannot tell you how many runs I've missed by not heeding this advice and feeling guilty. When I follow this, I not only accomplish my goal but achieve a sense of pride.

Now the harder part—changing your eating habits. Write down what you know you will need for nourishment—fruits, vegetables, and whole foods that cleanse you, do not weigh you down, and make you feel sluggish. Take the list to the grocery store and buy only what is on the list. And avoid what you should not be eating. This will be a challenge for most—myself included—as we cannot help but avoid the comfort foods that don't serve our greater good. Just try it. Better yet, just do it!

Just take the first step, and once you are in motion, your motivation and drive will continue. But, of course, to make it all happen and the way you want life to be, you must meditate daily in order to achieve it all and more.

Affirmations

- I focus on the things I can do and make them even better.
- My choices are for my greater good.
- When I start to believe I can't, I remind myself I am capable of anything I set out to do.

PATHWAY 4

Accepting You Are Good Enough

Be gentle with yourself. You are a child of the universe, no less than the trees and the stars; you have a right to be here.

—Max Ehrmann

Some days turn out better than others, which gives us the balance of good and bad days. But ultimately, the way we *feel* about our lives and ourselves has the biggest impact on the outcome of each day. Happiness and confidence can create outcomes that exceed our expectations, like a continual ray of sunshine even on a cloudy day.

But when we are down on ourselves and think we are not good enough, life can quickly take a turn for the worse. We can unexpectedly find ourselves deep in a dark hole. When we allow ourselves to feel this way for days, weeks, or even months at a time, it can have a damaging impact on our happiness and lead to depression as well as a decline in our physical health. There are also physical consequences associated with prolonged negativity. If we are depressed and anxious, we are also under emotional and physical stress. Stress kills. It leads to heart disease, sleeplessness, inertia, eating disorders, etc.

That is why it is best to prevent a *self-esteem slide*. Sometimes the smallest bit of inspiration can help turn things around when we feel we are not good enough.

Reasons You Are Good Enough

Accept that perfection is unreachable.

No one can possibly be perfect; that is what makes us human. You can be happy that being imperfect makes you different than everyone else. Being perfect would make everyone identical. Our imperfections are what make us unique and special in this world. Therefore, be the perfect human being by being imperfect.

Learn to say no.

When you are doing your best to be perfect, it is hard to tell people no. You want to be the perfect spouse, sibling, or friend. However, taking on more and more things does not make you perfect or even a better person—it makes you more stressed.

Saying no is not only good for your mental health, but it is good for others as well. Many times, people will have to deal with their own issues, which will make them grow into stronger human beings, allowing them a chance to grow.

Try new things, even if you fail.

Being a perfectionist makes it difficult to try something new and different because of the fear of not doing it right. That takes the fun out of trying something new. Remaining stagnant is not healthy for anyone. Embrace your mistakes and move on.

Let some things go.

We tend to prioritize things that are not really important. Will you remember doing the dishes or having fun with your friends? Will you remember filing or having a great conversation with your coworker? When you learn to let the unimportant things go, you have more time for what matters most.

Life Is about Progress, Not Perfection

Striving for perfection is not necessarily a bad thing. Reaching higher and working harder to get what you want is certainly encouraged. However, it can be rather difficult to attain and you will always be striving to be perfect. This may leave you feeling like you are not good enough, especially in a world where the race toward perfectionism usually involves losing who you truly are while becoming what others think you should be.

Instead, strive for excellence, which is more attainable while *you* create the level of personal excellence that works best for you. Most of us are juggling so many tasks in so many areas of life that we cannot possibly be perfect in every area and still be happy. We attain excellence because it is far more rewarding than being perfect.

Do Something Now for a Better Outcome in This Moment

Nothing is written in stone except for the past, which cannot be changed. But we *can* change the way we feel about it. We cannot truly predict the future because now is forever changing based on what we do at each moment.

The best way to move forward is to be present and focus on the now in a positive manner. When we feel good, we give gratitude for what we have, allowing for even better to come to us.

The same is true when we focus on negative; however, positive thinking is much more powerful. No matter what happened, be grateful you are here, able to correct it and move forward—even if only in your mind where you process all the events in your life. For now, take a deep breath and, while exhaling, focus on the good and allow yourself the ability to help create a better outcome.

Positive Thinking Is Your Birthright

No matter what situation you are in, positive thinking can and will always come to your rescue but only if you allow it. The power of being positive is a gift to us all from Divine energy. Divine energy is positive energy.

If you want things to turn around for your highest good, you must keep your faith, release your fears, and keep your focus on solutions. Positive thinking is your birthright. It can always improve any situation, no matter how critical it may appear to be. Calming your negative inner dialogue by learning to recognize it is one way to do this. Self-affirmation is another. Associating with positive people (and avoiding negative people) is still another. Other people are naturally attracted to people with a positive vibe. There is almost a sort of magnetism, and there is an equally powerful repulsion to negative energy.

There Is More Right with You Than Wrong

Even during your struggles, do not forget to focus on your strengths. Too often our culture looks at each other's *weaknesses* and focuses on improving them. While having a balanced mind, body, and soul is important, some of our weaknesses exist to balance some of our greatest strengths.

When we switch our focus to what is right about ourselves, we can probably write a long list of things we wish to change. In the areas you would like to improve, be honest with yourself and if an area needs improving, create action steps to do so. You will come to know that there is more right with you than will ever be wrong.

We All Make Mistakes

The real truth about mistakes is that they are opportunities to teach us something and allow us to grow. If someone pitches you a ball and you drop it, you have not failed; you produced a result—a perceived mistake. You can wallow forever that your mistake produced an undesired result, or you can keep trying, trying, and trying again until you catch the ball more times than you drop it.

Mistakes point out our weaknesses so that we can grow stronger in whatever area we choose. We are constantly learning and growing while we are here. *Mistakes* are evidence that we are trying and doing the best we can.

When we continually learn and grow from our mistakes, we begin to see bigger success in our lives, more fulfillment, and lasting happiness. Success takes practice, and mistakes are part of that practice.

You Are Where You Need to Be Right Now

It may not seem like it, but the entire Universe has arranged itself to create your life where it is right now. It may not be where you *want* to be at all times, but the proof is that you are here now—right now. We all experience *bumps in the road*, but sometimes you have to go through a bumpy ride in order to get to the fields of success.

So, when you feel like you have failed or will never reach your goals, remind yourself that the Universe did not say *no*. It just said *not yet*. Remind yourself that you are in the perfect place right now and continue moving forward in faith.

Be Kind and Gentle with Yourself—You Are Doing the Best You Can

You do not have to belittle yourself for not getting there fast enough or as fast as others say you should. As long as you know that at the end of the day you gave it your all, that is all any of us can truly do. Your light flickers, no matter how small the flame. It still shines in the darkest night.

Compare yourself to a flower. Each one blooms at its own pace and shows its unique beauty. Continue to reach for the light, allowing yourself to be nurtured—much like the flower, your life will bloom in its proper time.

You Deserve Unconditional Love and Forgiveness

Holding on to negative thoughts about yourself will not bring you justice. The grief and pain will only end up affecting you. Let go of the bitterness and resentments toward yourself or your situation. Remove the focus and attention off of the unwanted negative feelings.

Forgive yourself for the *mistakes* and allow you to love yourself no matter what, which will lead you to even more positive feelings of understanding, compassion, and appreciation and allow you to attract better and better experiences.

There's Always a Solution—Keep Searching

Sometimes you might feel like you have reached the end of the road. Lucky for you, there is always a path called faith where new solutions appear. It may be a simple solution and may only be a part of the solution that you need to put together. The puzzle pieces are always there for you to place together.

Only Compare and Compete with Yourself

As mentioned multiple times, there is no need to try to compete or catch up with those who are in your field. Be the best version of *you* that you can be right now. You have nothing to prove to anyone, especially yourself. Be the change you want to see in yourself, and the future will take care of itself—when it eventually becomes a *now*.

You Cannot Always Change Things—You Can Change the Way You Look at Things

The present moment was created as a collective manifestation of your past thoughts, words, and actions. This may be hard to accept at first because it puts all of the responsibility on you regarding your feelings, judgments, and opinions for all that you experienced up until now. This may cause you to question the reality that you have created; it may even make you feel like you are not good enough to handle your creative ability. For now, try and observe what has happened to you rather than judge it.

Times may have been tough. But know that you are tougher. Believe you are good enough to create the life you desire, and you know that you are good enough to make it through any situation. When this happens, the way you look at things suddenly changes. Before you know it, your reality positively changes. Be sure to meditate on this, and the achievements will follow.

Now, who was it that said you are not good enough?

Affirmations

- I compare myself to no one but me.
- I always do the best I can in each moment.
- I don't have to be perfect, but I'm better than I used to be.

PATHWAY 5

Starting Your Dreams

There are only two mistakes one can make along the
road to truth; not going all the way, and not starting.

—Buddha

Being Aware

Many have made numerous starts and have confronted and overcome
some major hurdles. If you can identify your hurdles early in life, it
will be much easier to get started.

Some Obstacles That May Confront You:

Lack of drive.

The drive to pursue your heart's longing will emerge only when
you recognize and accept that you are not passionate about what
you are currently doing. If this is the current situation of your life, it
means that you must take a course of action. When you stop being

content and acknowledge that your life is not exciting, you will feel an overwhelming need to take that first step toward your dreams.

Do you enjoy how you spend your time? Do you feel as if you are making the impact you want? If not, it is time to make a shift.

Risk of failure.

Big long-term goals with microlevel planning may sound like they will cover it all for you. They do just the opposite. They create a feeling of fear in your heart even before you make the start. They can be so overwhelming that they prevent you from even starting.

It is not wise to get caught up in long-term plans at any stage of your project. A better approach is to focus on the small steps that connect you to your passion and dreams while keeping in mind the end result.

It is best to visualize short-term goals in order to achieve your long-term mission. It recommends working toward a two- or three-week goal while evaluating what you have achieved along the way.

This helps you respond to change quickly and allows you to create value at a greater speed. When you are creating value every week, every day, no matter how small it is—rather than achieving something tangible a year down the line—you will be motivated nonstop. You will stop considering failure at all because you will experience small successes at every step of the way.

Lack of clarity.

Often, we have clear dreams but hazy thinking on how to convert those dreams into reality. We get so busy with our day-to-day living that we do not make the time to think about what steps we need to take.

Until you create the time to think about what you want and need to do, you will keep spinning in circles within your head, waiting for the day when you suddenly feel enlightened and/or prepared. Remember what Buddha said: "We become what we think."

Only when we are thinking consciously will our thoughts carry the power to make it all happen.

Need of perfection.

The perfect time, the perfect method, the perfect idea—these are all illusions and excuses that keep us from reaching our dreams. When the kids grow up, when I get my next promotion, when I have more money, when I feel worthy, and so on … These are nothing more than ways of procrastinating. When my child's summer vacation is over … When I finish this project … The list never ends.

Oftentimes, these are lies we tell ourselves to avoid taking the plunge. There is no such thing as a perfect idea or a perfect method. Many ideas can be effective if we back them with a sense of purpose and then learn and adjust as we go.

Fear of letting go.

Maybe you have devoted years to training in your field and building a career only to realize you are not passionate about your work. This can make it challenging to let go and walk away. After all, you have already spent a good part of your life pursuing your profession, increasing your earning potential, and making a name for yourself.

You might feel highly resistant to abandoning that profession and pursuing something else. You may also think it is equivalent to accepting and declaring that your work and life this far were a waste.

The only thing that is wasteful is denying what you really want.

Living your life on your terms starts with living consciously and courageously and being true to yourself. It may mean letting go of the things you have collected and unlearning all that you have learned until now; it may mean fighting a long battle; it may even mean holding on to your belief in the face of criticism, disapproval, and discouragement. But it is worth doing.

So, go ahead and crush the fears, let go of the doubts, overpower the ones who say you can't do it, and take that one leap of faith to be who you want to be—no matter what your age, gender, culture, or boundaries are.

Affirmation

- I start and finish my goals in a timely manner.

PATHWAY 6

Taking Control of Your Life

Your life begins to change the day you take responsibility for it.
—Steve Maraboli

Ways to Take Back Control of Your Life

Ask yourself this question: If you had to relive your life all over again, without being able to change anything, would you want to?

Most people believe that life just happens to them, and they have no control over the outcome. As stated earlier, everything happens for a reason. However, you can take charge of your reality and shape it based on the power of your thoughts and actions at the present time— more so if you have felt frustrated and unhappy with the direction of your life up until now.

Tips to Help You Take Charge of Your Life Starting Today:

Realize that life is not happening to you; it is responding to you.

The energy you give out begins within your own mind; if you think positive thoughts, you will start seeing positive things happening right before your eyes and, of course, vice versa.

Think of your mind as a factory where your future is manufactured based on what you think. Every time you have a negative thought and you repeat in your mind, you are asking for that to produce, and it has no choice but to exist. Therefore, your reality is manufactured based on what you repeatedly think of and the kind of realities materialize from those thoughts.

Start thinking positive thoughts so you can function at a much higher level.

Do not ever give your power away to anything outside of yourself.

Instead of taking responsibility for our lives, many of us find it easier and more convenient to place blame on things or people outside ourselves. If we do not like our job, we blame our bosses rather than ourselves for choosing a job we do not enjoy. If we get sick, we blame others for spreading the illness rather than ourselves for not taking care of our immune system. Just note how many times a day you give away your power to things outside yourself. You might be surprised by what you will find. Once you accept and take charge of who you are, no person, place, or thing outside of yourself will ever overpower you.

Listen to your own heart.

Other people can offer their opinions about what direction your life should take, but you get to make the ultimate decision. Because you know your heart's desires better than anyone else, wouldn't it be unfair to you to let others decide for you? The only way to live an authentic, purposeful life is through your own heart, so start listening to what it tells you to do while taking action at the same time.

Know it's okay to say no.

Taking command of your life means getting honest with yourself about what activities and friends bring about your best self and which ones no longer serve you. This way, you will give yourself room to say yes to activities and people that actually serve your best interest and elevate you and your consciousness.

Master your own health.

If you have your health, you have everything. Make a promise with yourself to practice a healthier, more wholesome lifestyle that includes lots of real food (such as raw fruits and vegetables), clean water, good healthy sleep, and moderate exercise. By making small changes each day, you can transform your health and at the same time increase your energy and vibration of your frequency. Honor your body and choose foods and drinks that will give you a long, healthy life.

Look for a new job if you want.

None of us came to this world just because; we came here to *change* the world. If your job makes you feel like it is just another day of life and does not allow you to follow your true purpose, do not think twice about leaving it behind. We live in a world where money is needed and where we must pay to survive at the moment and in the future. Plenty of people have created their own jobs that you too can do. Think about how liberating it would feel to do something you love and still get paid for it.

Forget about the normal, everyday things.

If you really want to take charge of your life, you will have to get comfortable with living to the beat of your own drum. Too many people fall prey just because it feels safe, not because it feels right. They fear others judging them and do not want to become alienated or ridiculed. However, even if it feels lonely at first, you will never know what lies ahead if you never take the chance and make the journey. Create your life on your terms and do not worry what others think. You did not come here to blend in. You were born to stand out!

Do more of what makes you happy.

Many people shy away from new opportunities or activities because they fear failure or they live in fear of what others think. Both of these fears can imprison you; do not allow them to stand in the way of whatever makes you happy. The longer you wonder about the outcome, the more time you waste ruminating instead of living. Really living with intention means taking charge of your own happiness, so take action and start following what makes you happy.

Live within your means.

This one can totally restore your life because you will have to look at what you truly need as opposed to what you want. Do you really need to go shopping for new clothes every week? Do you absolutely need that new iPhone, or can you still use the one you currently have? Many spend way more than what they earn and then feel stressed out because of their financial situations. Sell or donate what you do not really need and only buy things that add to your well-being. In due time, you will learn to understand what is needed and what is not.

Become more mindful.

Meditating will help; becoming more aware of yourself and the universe will teach you to take full responsibility for yourself and what happens to you. It will give you discipline and mental strength and take you out of the habit of living on autopilot. As the master of your reality, you must take full responsibility for the quality of the life you lead. Cultivating more awareness will allow you to move forward into creating your life instead of watching passively from the sidelines.

Are you ready to take your life back?

Affirmation

- I am in control of my own destination. I am making a positive transformation.

PATHWAY 7

Moving Ahead with Change

Once you make a decision, the universe
conspires to make it happen.
—Ralph Waldo Emerson

Desire for Change

Have you ever had an inner knowing that it was time to make some life changes, but you felt too confused and scared to make them? I have certainly felt that way many times. After I graduated from college years ago, I felt completely confused about what I was going to do with my life. I was asking myself questions like: How am I going to find meaning? What should I do for a career? How can I make my dreams a reality?

Diana: I remember one cloudy night, lying in bed reading fiction books for hours. I wanted to escape from the nonstop confusion and endless, pointless questions running through my mind. The reality is I was apprehensive as to what my future held. I was scared to start a job, yet scared not to. I did not want to move away from the comforts of home, yet I could not wait to get out. I was scared of the unknown, but I was also excited by the fact that anything good could happen. I was afraid to make a change, so I tricked myself into thinking that it was too complicated and confusing. For a couple of months, I did nothing, and my frustration grew as days and months passed.

Fear with confusion happens when you have an inner knowing that things are *off* or you want to make a major life change, but you feel too uneasy to take action. In other words, this is fear-based confusion. It seems like there are too many problems, unknowns, reasons, why nots, or decisions that are too difficult to make. So, staying in a state of confusion is easier to deal with.

Does this sound familiar to you? Maybe you are confused about making a career change, moving to a new city, ending a relationship, or getting your finances in order. We've all experienced this kind of fear with confusion in one form or another and know how frustrating it can be. There is a way out of this fear-based trap, however.

Acknowledge Your Fear

Luckily, fear that grips us with confusion is easy to move beyond. First and foremost, the fear itself must be acknowledged. We cannot rid ourselves of any problem before we define it as a problem. Below are some ways to move through life's confusions and finally get clear on what you want.

Follow Your Excitement

If the fear runs deep, following your excitement will help. For example, instead of trying to answer the question, *What should I do with my life?* ask yourself, *What excites me right now?* Make a list of all the activities and experiences that excite you now. Try not to judge or rewrite your list to justify how you may be perceived. Just be open and honest with yourself as to what excites *you*. If walking to a local cafe for some homemade chai tea each morning is something enjoyable, add it to your list. There is nothing too small or insignificant here. If you enjoy it, add it!

There are benefits to following what excites you in this moment. You will start to feel more excited about your life. Your excitement will also lead you to people and experiences that will help you set a direction for yourself. Follow what excites you and know that you will feel a shift in your mood as you change and grow.

Following your excitement now is easier than trying to figure out your whole life. Your life will take care of itself as it unfolds; one moment at a time. In addition, it leaves room for expansion and gives you the freedom to continually try new things.

Deciding Your Direction

Right now, make a choice as to what it is you desire. Making a clear decision is the quickest way out of confusion. This may sound obvious, but sometimes we have silly inner thoughts that hold us back. Thoughts like, *I am not good enough, I do not deserve this, I am never lucky*, and so on.

But you most definitely are good enough, and you do deserve peace and all that comes with life no matter what you are telling yourself. Believe in yourself enough to know that you will make the right choice. Express to yourself your heart's desire and expect it to take place. Do not be concerned about a bad decision because there is no such thing. In my opinion, making no decision at all is often the worst decision to make.

For me, sinking deeper into my confusion, I decided to pack a backpack and took a hiking trip with friends. I had no idea if that would help me answer my big life questions, but it excited me.

When returned home from that trip, I felt confident and even more excited. I then made a concrete decision about my future, and that completely changed everything for me. The point is it did not really matter what I did. Rather, it was my initial decision to do something that got me out of my confusion.

Once you make the initial decision and take action, the Universe will start to provide you with people and experiences that help you move forward. So, breathe, become aware of how your decision feels in your body, and act on whatever feels good and pure to you.

Letting Go of Outcomes

Expectations lead to disappointment. When we finally make the decision to change, we come up with a detailed plan for how it should all turn out. We immediately search for something that will make us feel secure in the face of change only to elude us.

But the truth is you can manifest much quicker when you open yourself up to all the possibilities that you have not yet thought of— ones that may have never crossed your mind.

Not only is it okay to focus on what you want, but it is the first step toward manifesting. Simply focus on what excites you right now. How does that make you feel in this moment? If you experience joy, then continue to focus on that. This allows you to feel joy at the moment, regardless of the outcome in the future.

You are meant to be here right now. The proof of that is that you are! As you focus on following what excites you in this moment, the fuzziness of confusion begins to clear, and you can see in what direction you are heading. Then, moving forward with inner confidence becomes natural.

But do know that it is okay to feel unsafe in the process. Experience teaches that the vulnerability associated with change is completely worth it. You are worth more than you can imagine. Do not let the confusion or frustration hold you back more than it has already. Once you take the first step, everything else will unfold for you in the blink of an eye.

So, take that first step toward a better life so you can live life to the best of your ability.

Affirmation

- Right now, I take the first step and move ahead with what feels right in this moment—regardless of the results.

PATHWAY 8

Your Intuition

I walk away from projects if it doesn't feel right … it
could be a great idea, but the script doesn't work.

—Blair Underwood

Ways to Tune into Your Intuition

Your intuition, commonly known as your gut feelings or inner guide, is an instinct—a knowing of something to be true or false without any supportive evidence. In other words, you just know.

Many of the great thinkers consider intuition a major part of our thought process and our connection to the subconscious mind. It is the best source for tapping into our creativity and wisdom. When we trust our intuition, it can have a great impact on our lives, allowing us to tap into our full potential.

Always Trust Your Gut Instincts

You know the feeling you get when something is not quite right, yet logic says do it anyway? Well, that is your gut warning you. Chances are you have gone against your gut a time or two and wished you had trusted instead.

Trusting your intuition can be scary, especially when all the logical evidence points to the contrary. When something does not feel quite right, it probably is not.

Make a commitment to trust your gut feelings. The only way to learn to trust it is to take that first step. When you realize it will not let you down, you will be more willing to trust it in the future.

Learn to Listen with Open Ears

Listening to your intuition in a noisy world can be a challenge. When you are struggling, you have the perfect opportunity to consult your greatest teacher—your inner guide. To do that, though, you need to learn to listen to it.

It is important to quiet the noise around you and focus on how you feel about the question at hand. Let go of the desire to analyze, compare, and examine the issue. Just listen and tap into your feelings. When you are actively listening to your intuition, the answer will become clear.

Pay Close Attention

So much of our days are made up of habitual behaviors—behaviors that require little to no thought at all. If we are moving through our day using habits, then we are not allowing ourselves to tap into intuition.

An important part of developing intuition is paying attention to what is happening around us. Our intuition uses information our conscious minds gather through interaction and experience. The more information our conscious minds gather, the more insightful our intuition becomes.

Remember Your Dreams

Our subconscious minds talk to us not only through our gut feelings but also through our dreams. Once you begin to pay attention to your dreams, you will gain very valuable insight into your life. Recalling dreams can be hard at times, but it will become easier when you train your brain to reflect on them first thing in the morning. Better yet, if the dream wakes you up, write them down immediately.

You can use your dreams to help put your intuitive guide to work. Before you go to sleep, consider the challenges that are still unsolved. Spend a few minutes thinking about possible solutions. This will help trigger your inner guide to continue working while you are sleeping. Make sure you use the Dream Control Technique to bring you better success when searching for a solution, which can be found in the Silva Centering Exercise section.

Make sure you have a journal next to your bed. When you awaken in the morning, you can write down your first thoughts and record the dreams you had. You might be surprised to find some creative solutions coming to you through your dreams.

Meditate Daily

There is no greater way to tap into your inner guide than through meditation. Meditation can be a scary word to many people who don't understand it, but there is nothing to be afraid of. Meditation is all about quieting the outside noise and excessive mental self-talk so the important messages can come through.

Start by just focusing on your breathing for a minute or two. There is no wrong way to meditate; it simply is what it is. The key here is to become focused on allowing your intuition to speak to you.

Start by asking for inner guidance around an issue you are having. Sit still and focus your mind to allow you to tap into the wisdom of your intuition. When you ask a specific question, and you are ready to receive an answer, your intuition will make it clear for you.

Developing and trusting your intuition is a skill. Start small and continue to practice it to build up your intuitive muscles. The more you choose to listen and act upon your inner guide, the better you will follow what your gut feelings tell you to do.

Affirmation

- I meditate often and pay close attention to what my intuition tells me. I use these gifts for the greater good of everyone and everything I encounter.

PATHWAY 9

Serenity Now

Serenity comes when you trade expectations for acceptance.
—Buddha

Things Will Never Be Perfect; Therefore, Make Peace with Everyday Challenges

Diana: A few weeks ago, I walked into my house and found it quite a mess, with a lot of cleaning to be done … from clothes on the floor to dishes on the couch to paper scattered everywhere. It had been one of those weeks when things were all going well, but there seemed to be no time for household chores.

I looked around, took a deep breath, moved a pizza box out of the way, enjoyed dinner with my family, and then went to bed. I got up the next morning feeling rested and straightened up the house joyfully. Before long, the whole family was cleaning with me.

Why am I telling you this? You see, a few months prior I would have stressed out and felt totally guilty about the house being such a mess. I would have gone into an entire inner negative conversation with myself about how I was not organized enough and how I could not keep things together.

This would have led me into a cleaning obsession for the rest of the night, and I would have gone to bed feeling tired and depleted, waking up the next morning in an exhausting state of mind.

When I first opened the door, I chose to fully accept and be at peace with what was rather than beat myself up with idealistic expectations of how I thought things should be.

It was a subtle yet important shift in my life. I approached the situation calmly, and rather than feeling bad about the clutter, I simply acknowledged that the house needed to be cleaned.

Yes, there were clothes thrown on the floor. Yes, I had been working many hours and did not have the time to do laundry. I also acknowledged that *messy* was a relative term, and I realized that I felt a bit of shame about having a disorderly place because of strict rules I grew up with.

I accepted the fact that the house was the way it was and that it was okay to not do anything at that very moment. It was so simple. In just a few moments, I suddenly felt myself breathing easier as a result and sleeping a lot better without the worry and inner thoughts playing over and over in my mind.

Sometimes we need to accept what is so that we can find peace of mind no matter what kind of day we are having or what type of circumstance we encounter.

Peace is available to us, even when life seems to be out of our control. It may not feel like it, but beyond confusion is serenity, if we only accept it. Solutions to our problems are also clearer when we move into this place of peace.

When Stressing about Doing Things Now or Later, Remind Yourself of the Following Five Things:

1. Acknowledge what is here. Simply notice for a few seconds what you are feeling, experiencing, seeing, and hearing without any judgment. Also, notice if any judgment is coming from other people in your life.

2. Accept that each situation fully as it is supposed to be. No shame, no guilt—just acceptance and lots of deep breaths.

3. Be open to the inner wisdom that you possess. There may not be an immediate solution, and that is totally fine. Sometimes a break is just what we need before we take the next step in life.

4. Remember that you are enough just as you are. It is a beautiful thing to accept the fullness of your human experience rather than wishing it were something else.

5. There will always be homes to clean, items on the to-do list, obligations to meet, inboxes to clear, and schedules to make. In the middle of all that, there will always be peace and joy available to us if we simply notice.

May you find the highest serenity as you let go of expectations and fully accept yourself and your life experiences.

Affirmation

- I always find serenity in all moments in my life—even if things are not yet the way I would like them to be.

PATHWAY 10

Facing Your Fears, One Step at a Time

Take that first step. Bravely overcoming one small
fear gives you the courage to take on the next.

—Daisaku Ikeda

Taking Small Steps to Do the Thing That Scares You the Most

Diana: When I was young, I loved to climb monkey bars and trees, but I was always too scared to get down by myself. Somehow, when standing at the base of a massive oak tree, I had forgotten how terrified I felt at the top.

I climbed the highest I could climb, trying to prove to all the kids in the neighborhood that I was fearless and then staying up while being there for ten minutes, which was forever at that age. But instead, I was clutching the bark and crying until someone helped me safely reach the ground.

I was a daredevil tomboy who was adventurous and tough, but I was deathly afraid of feeling out of control and getting hurt.

You can probably imagine how terrified I felt when skydiving some years ago. It was a lot higher than the tree branches, making the rise to the top a lot more terrifying. Still, I wanted to do it. Though I had a whole list of reasons not to …

- I wanted to prove to myself that I could do it all.
- I wanted to feel alive and free when falling.
- I wanted to face a fear, and the thought of overcoming it was exciting.
- I wanted to impress and inspire myself that I could do it.
- I wanted to impress my best friend, who had invited me in the first place.

It would have been easy to psych myself out of going. It was the scariest thing I had ever done. I was overwhelmed with emotion and even slightly paralyzed to a certain point. It did not help matters that someone tweeted me a link to skydiving fatalities an hour before my best friend showed up.

In that moment, it seemed far more reasonable to back out. I knew it was unlikely that I would drop dead from jumping, but even the slightest risk seemed too big to take.

As I read through the various stories of things that had gone wrong for others, wrestling with my fear of facing a similar fate, I reminded myself that the part of me that wanted to do it was greater than the part of me that was afraid.

I realized the only way I would follow through was to stop thinking and focus on doing. I had to start moving toward it—one step at a time.

I told myself that all I had to do was get in the car at ten o'clock that morning. At that moment, none of the other steps mattered. I did not have to deal with those fears right then; I just had to deal with the task that was in front of me, which was to get there.

After that, all I had to do was walk to the entrance, one foot in front of the other. Then, all I had to do was dress up and ready myself for the jump.

Though it was a challenge, I chose not to fill any of those moments with the fear of falling. I did not have to concern myself with how I would feel in moments to come. I just had to be in the present, doing the simple tasks it required.

Eventually, I got to the point where all I had to do was board the plane.

That is when I started crying—in front of strangers who did not seem to be or even appear slightly nervous.

Yes, I felt emotion. Yes, I expressed it visibly. But, no, it did not stop me. Okay, it almost did.

After my best friend barreled out excitedly, like a kid doing a cannonball in a swimming pool, my tandem diver pushed me to the open door. I could almost feel the bark under my fingernails as I clutched to the sides for safety. That was the moment I had not thought through—all the tiny steps that led me there.

The horrifying terror I felt right then was what I had feared the most. I likely would not have gotten to that point if I had started feeling it far sooner than necessary.

What I did was focus on each tiny step until I was face-to-face with the most frightening one, and then, with nothing left to do, I took a deep breath and jumped and landed, panting, laughing, crying, and feeling more alive than ever before.

This, I have realized, is one of the most effective ways to do anything that scares us—by focusing on one step at a time without dreading how we will feel later in the process.

If you put too much attention on things that could go wrong later, you limit your effectiveness right now. That is not to say you shouldn't plan to avoid potential problems. It's just that if you function in a state of constant anxiety, it will eventually weaken you.

Whatever it is you want to do, it does not need to be a massive, overwhelming goal. Instead, think of it as a series of steps, some simpler than others; therefore, one should commit to completing at least some of the simpler steps every day.

Absorb yourself completely in each phase as you move forward, giving it your full attention as if nothing else matters but what you are in that moment, as if showing up for each part of the journey is in itself the goal.

It does not matter if you are on a hard path. It does not matter if the odds are against you. It does not matter if you are not making progress as quickly as others are.

All that matters is that you take a step and keep taking them, even if you do not know where they are leading you.

Jumping into something new can be terrifying. You never know where you are going to land until you get there, and it is hard to silence your fears about just where that may be.

It is okay to feel scared. Just know it does not have to control you—not if you choose to focus on where you are and put your heart into the step of the moment.

For years, I told myself I was not who I wanted to be because I felt so scared. I have since realized it is not my fear of falling that defines me. It is the fact that I am willing to make the climb in spite of all the feelings it brings up.

What tiny, manageable step can you take today toward what scares you the most?

Affirmation

- I focus on each present moment when challenging my fears by taking small steps to achieve my goals.

PATHWAY 11

Positive Thinking

You can't be both awesome and negative. Choose one.
—Karen Salmansohn

Habits That Stop Negative Thinking

Contrary to traditional belief, life is not merely a random sequence of events that involuntarily happen to us. Our thoughts, words, and actions largely create what happens to us. We have the incredible power to help mold our minds so that we can begin to master our lives.

However, many people struggle with how to do this in the long term. They might practice it for a while and then lose interest and go back to old, doubtful, negative thinking ways and patterns. If you want to stop harmful, negative thoughts in their tracks and learn how to cultivate a positive mind, try out the following tips in your own life.

Focus on One Positive Affirmation

Like the saying goes, one thing at a time. Trying to do and think of everything at once can be overwhelming and lead to stress, which is what we're looking to get rid of. Instead of repeating many positive things, focus on just one. The mind can have trouble juggling many different positive affirmations in one day, so give your mind a break and tell it just one at a time. It can be something simple, such as, "I love myself." Anytime you feel something negative come up, release it and replace the bad energy with positive words.

Do this throughout the day when your mind tends to bring up demeaning thoughts about yourself. It takes practice, but incorporate this method every day for a month, and you will see a drastic difference and change in your thinking patterns.

Keep Busy with Anything That Enhances Your Life

If you have too much time on your hands, your mind wanders simply because you have nothing to occupy it. The mind needs to engage in tasks or activities in order to retain sharpness and vibrancy. You can work out, hang out with positive and uplifting people, volunteer at your local animal shelter or community garden, or go to yoga classes—anything you enjoy that promotes positivity in your life.

Staying busy will keep toxic thoughts under control and put your mind into a state of flow, so you have something to do other than overthinking.

Keep a Gratitude Journal

If you listen to successful, happy people on the planet today, they usually have a grateful and humble attitude toward life. They express gratitude each morning for seemingly insignificant things, like having headphones to listen to music, having a floor to walk on, having eyes to see, or whatever else comes into their stream of consciousness. They list or simply acknowledge every little thing they feel thankful for and allow that energy to carry over into the rest of the day.

When you awaken in the morning and go to sleep in the evening, be in silence and write everything you feel blessed by in life. This can make a world of difference in how you perceive your world and yourself.

Transform Negative Thinking into Positive

Looking on the bright side of the most tragic situations can really pay off at the end of the day. If you get in a wreck that totals your car, feel thankful you lived to see your loved ones again. If someone stole your wallet, look at everything else you still have that others may not. You can look at any situation you encounter and take away something positive from it, but you have to adjust your attitude first. How you see the world reflects the way you see yourself. Once you cultivate a positive outlook about yourself, you will see your environment entirely differently. Colors will get brighter, people will seem friendlier, and the world will just seem like a more beautiful, happier place. Find the beauty within and see the beauty without.

Ask Yourself if Your Current Thoughts Are Helping or Hurting

Do your thoughts serve your best interests, helping you create positive results without resistance? Do they nourish your mind and spirit or make you feel inadequate and powerless? Observe your normal thinking patterns without judgment and decide if you need to develop new thinking habits. Chances are, most of your thoughts are probably not helping you.

Most people's thoughts run on autopilot until they start paying attention to them. Once you do, you can retrain your brain to think positively by practicing affirmations and only repeating the uplifting, nourishing thoughts to yourself. Discard the negative thoughts after you have observed them and thanked them for their presence; they can still teach you lessons, but they should not have a permanent residence in your brain.

Do you prefer to practice these negative-thinking stoppers or positive affirmations that will help you live the life of your dreams?

Affirmation

- I choose positive thoughts that allow me to feel better about myself and the world.

PATHWAY 12

The Joy of the Journey

The journey is the reward.

—Chinese Proverb

You Will Not Be the Same Person When You Achieve Your Goal

When you set goals, you naturally focus on the result, keeping the end in mind. However, if you pay attention to the desired achievement, you will discover the path to getting there. The value you gain from achieving the goal is not just about the reward of accomplishment.

Once you reach a specific goal, you are not the person you started as on your journey. The actual process of achieving along with the experience you gain will have changed you. The journey is the reward.

If you set the goal of losing forty pounds and you get there, you will have gained more than the results of looking good and having spiked interest from others. Yes, the reward is the finished product, but the actual effort of doing it is gratifying.

In order to reduce the weight, you need to lead a very disciplined and focused lifestyle. You need to take charge of your eating habits and ensure you do not lapse into your old ways. You need to work out regularly and efficiently, and you will actually make serious gains when working out.

A great body is not just a thing you have; it is a lifestyle you lead. Adopting that lifestyle is the key benefit.

How many people make the necessary sacrifices and do the hard work required to lose serious weight? Not nearly as many as the number who set the goal. Taking those steps changes both the mind and body.

The reward is not just the tangible change in your body. It is the journey that has given you improved discipline and willpower.

Exactly the same applies to the goal of quitting your job and running your own business. Everyone dreams about it, but very few people take charge. Those who are successful have not just won the prize of being their own boss and earning a better income.

The long hours they have worked, the risks they have taken with their time and money, and the fear and uncertainty they have experienced about whether it would work out all amount to the desired changes.

Diana: It took me years of working on my coaching business before it earned me enough money to kiss the desk goodbye. The money is not the prize; it is the time and freedom I now have. But if those things had just fallen into my lap without any effort or sacrifice on my behalf, I would not be able to appreciate them in the same manner.

I would still have been the same person I used to be.

No doubt the time and freedom are great. But when I really think about the process I went through, I recognize that the changes in me as a person have provided greater value in the long term. I dreamed big, I devoted many hours, and I was feared that it would all be a waste. But I just put one foot in front of the other, moving forward with each step, and eventually I reached my goal.

Thanks to the journey, I internalized the success process, which is the greatest reward—to know that I can reach a goal by pointing myself in the right direction and taking small and gradual action. I now have utter faith that little by little, I am making progress, even if it does not appear that way, and I can succeed if I just stick to the task.

The person you become when you reach a significant goal is a person who is more likely to achieve future goals.

That is why people who are successful in one area are often successful in others. It is no surprise that many high-performing business people and executives are also extremely fit.

At first glance, it does not appear to be linked. But each require consistent action over a long period of time.

Personal development is not about having stuff. It is not about having a good body, a compatible partner, and a passive, free-flowing income. Those things may come, but they are signals of the changes you undertake on your journey.

The compatible partner is a signal that you have learned how to open yourself up, love, and be selfless. The passive, free-flowing income signals that you have learned how to provide value to the world and have chosen infinite possibility over security. The lean body signals that you nourish your physical temple with healthy food and can effectively challenge yourself with exercise.

The changes in yourself are much more deeply satisfying than the actual stuff you receive.

When you set goals for the purpose of developing yourself rather than a physical symbol of success, you are more likely to achieve it. You may need the physical symbol to drive you and measure your progress, but it is the journey that changes you and the journey that is the reward.

Even if you never actually achieve the physical goal, perhaps because you have changed your mind and changed course, that is actually a change in yourself, which is still a reward.

The physical signs of success are not required for growth to occur. They are merely reflections of that growth, along with intangible reflections, such as peace and fulfillment.

This idea that the journey is more important than the destination is a common sentiment. It just took me a while to figure out that it was true and really internalize it.

It is so easy to read stories and proverbs of profound wisdom, nod your head in agreement, but never really take them honestly. But a theoretical appreciation of wisdom is not enough; it needs to be internalized to become part of the fabric of your being.

So how do you internalize something? You simply have experiences. Put yourself in challenging situations, set yourself audacious goals, and meditate on statements of wisdom to apply them to your process.

If you chase experiences and not things, those experiences will change you, the wisdom gained will be internalized, and that will be your greatest reward.

Affirmation

- I enjoy the journey of reaching my goal as much as I enjoy achieving it.

PATHWAY 13

Goodbye to Excuses— Reclaiming Your Personal Power

People are always blaming their circumstances for what they are.
I don't believe in circumstances. The people who get on in this
world are the people who get up and look for the circumstances
they want, and, if they can't find them, make them.

—George Bernard Shaw

Take Back Your Power and Start Loving Your Life

Excuses. We all make them one after another. And we make them for everything all the time without even realizing it, pointing the finger at someone or something else—anything or anyone but ourselves. Most of us say, "I don't think I make excuses. Blaming people? Who me? No way!"

Diana: Once I took a real, hard look at my life, I realized I was full of excuses and blame for why I was always running late and why I could not start living a healthier life, do the dishes, go out on a Friday night, or return a phone call. I justified my reasons for why I could not do this or that, why I was not good enough, why my life was not what I wished it was, why my financial situation was not the best, why I was upset at someone, and so on.

You name it, and I had an excuse. I blamed everything and everyone for why I could not accomplish my goals, why I felt a certain way, and why I was not fulfilled or happy. Nothing was my fault or my responsibility. This was hard to see and even harder to finally admit.

What increased my self-awareness about the excuses I made was a cold, hard dose of reality when I had a fallout with my best friend, whom I've had since I was ten-years-old. I chose to leave because it did not feel right, but it left me shattered and heartbroken. It became painfully clear that I really had no idea who I was. I was forced to figure myself out. For the first time ever, I was being honest with myself—brutally honest, about everything. Before this happened, I had never once stopped to think about my choices and how they had affected my life and the people around me.

I used to think that life just happened, and I had no control over it. Things occurred as they did. Life was hard and unfair. It was not my fault that I was not happy or did not have what I thought I wanted or needed. It was the fault of those around me. Because I was not happy or fulfilled, I thought it was my best friend's fault. For years, I put that responsibility in her hands, yet I never took responsibility for my actions or myself.

By putting the responsibility of my happiness in her hands, I was setting us both up for friendship failure. Figuring this out was just the tip of the iceberg. It made me realize just how often I made excuses and passed blame in all areas of my life. No wonder I was not happy.

You may not think you make excuses or pass blame, but we all have—and many times it is done without knowing. You may even find yourself getting irritated when you notice other people behaving this way. I challenge you to start taking a look at yourself—pay attention to your choices, decisions, and reasons for doing or not doing certain things. You might be surprised to find just how many excuses you make on a day-to-day basis. Do not judge yourself. Just notice what comes up and really pay attention.

When we continue to make excuses and blame others, we are actually giving our power away. We are telling ourselves that we have no control over our behaviors, our decisions, our lives, or our feelings. That is just not true! When we blame others for what we are going through, we avoid responsibility and continue with the problem. Excuses hold us back from being the best we can be, being honest with ourselves, and living authentic lives.

I did not understand what any of this meant until I started taking responsibility for myself—all of myself and not just in parts. I took responsibility for thoughts, actions, decisions, and feelings. I practiced being honest with myself and continue to do so every day because it gives me the balance I seek. The keyword here is *practice*.

My best friend and I mended our ways, but things are different now. We are in a much better place than we were before. When we had the fallout, I learned so much about myself. Most importantly, I learned that the only person responsible for what happens to me is me.

Being honest with ourselves is not easy. It is hard to take the same finger we have been pointing at everyone else and turn it around to ourselves. We have to be compassionate and loving with ourselves. It is not easy to start looking at the parts of ourselves we are not proud of. It is not easy to admit how often we do these things. It is hard to take ownership of our mistakes and problems. Loving and accepting these parts of ourselves does not mean we did anything wrong.

I truly believe that we are always doing the best we can. Once we gain awareness of things we want to change about ourselves, we cannot turn around and be mad at ourselves for how we acted in the past. We can only make changes if we are good to ourselves. From there, we can start taking full responsibility for our lives instead of making excuses and blaming other people.

This can be hard to do, especially if there seems to be a valid reason to blame someone else. For example, say your significant other of many years has decided to leave you. Your world is shattered as a result of his or her actions. Yes, the person left. Yes, the person might have done something to hurt you. You can be sad, brokenhearted, and mad—but stop there! Do not let his or her actions ruin you and your life. You have the option to let the other person's decision define you, or you can accept what happened, feel all of your feelings (and grieve), take responsibility for yourself, pick up the pieces, and move forward.

If you let your life fall apart because of something someone else did, you are allowing yourself to be controlled. It's up to us to take situations like this and learn from them, let ourselves grow, and change. When I started practicing being totally honest with myself about my choices and my life, I realized that I am in control of my own happiness. This realization changed me. I actually started to really enjoy my life. Taking responsibility for my life forced me to start living it for real.

The only way we can truly be happy is to realize that our thoughts, emotions, actions, and decisions are our responsibility and no one else's. That is a beautiful thing. No more excuses. No more blame. Just the choice to take our power back and start living and loving our lives to the fullest we choose.

Affirmation

- I choose to be fully responsible for all that I am and make no excuses for any perceived shortcomings.

PATHWAY 14

Everyday Feelings

Every day may not be good, but there's
something good in every day.
—Alice Morse Earle

Releasing Bad Moods

Contrary to popular belief, positive people have bad moods.

Maybe you didn't get enough sleep last night. You feel overworked and overwhelmed. Perhaps something happened, and you keep dwelling on it—going over and over in your head how you froze up at a meeting or how you spoke too aggressively to someone you love. Maybe you dropped your cell phone in a kitchen sink full of water.

Whatever it is, you feel something you do not want to feel, and you are not sure how to change it. You just know you need to do something before acting on those feelings.

The reality is you do not have to act on everything you feel. Still, emotional responses happen so quickly that it becomes challenging to put space between feeling and doing.

It may seem like the answer is to stop responding to life emotionally, but that is just not realistic. Actually, it is nearly impossible to bypass an emotional response because of the way our brains are set up.

Identifying negative feelings quickly instead of responding to those feelings with more negative feelings helps improve your state of mind. Odds are, if you choose to retaliate, you will do something you will regret later.

Steps to Overcoming a Negative Mind

Get to the root.

Have you ever snapped at someone who said something to offend you?

You're probably familiar with this common dilemma—and when it happens, you either fly off the handle or become quiet with negative thoughts flowing, so you start looking for explanations. The kids are too loud, the television is too small, the cars are too dirty, and so on.

Maybe you are afraid of acknowledging that you hurt someone because you prefer to avoid confrontation. Or, maybe you are disappointed in yourself, but admitting is too painful.

Whatever the case may be, it is time to get honest.

Lashing out at others will not solve the problems that are creating your feelings, much less lashing out at yourself.

Be real.

There is no point in pretending you are full of sunshine when internally you feel like crying or screaming. You are entitled to feel the full range of emotions and express what is on your mind when you need to. Allow yourself to feel those emotions—whatever they may be. Do not worry about bringing other people down; you will only do that if you dwell in negativity.

If someone asks what is wrong, be honest. Tell them, "I've had a rough day. I don't feel so great, but I'm sure I'll feel better when I …"

Complete the sentence: "I'll feel better when I …"

Everyone has something that is guaranteed to put a smile on his or her face. Playing with a puppy might bring you joy. Watching reruns of *Friends* might make you laugh. Dancing to enlightening music might be wonderful and fun to do.

Doing something fun to shift the energy is the best way to make a day better. It is helpful to have these kinds of ideas, which, in turn, will put a smile on your face when most needed.

Diana: Yoga always enhances my mood. But one thing I know for sure is that when I feel bad, I am less motivated to workout. But it helps if I remind myself that it will be worth it in the long run if I push through my discomfort. Yoga always allows me to release body stress from the inside out.

Take responsibility.

Sometimes when you are down, it might feel like you have to stay there. But the truth is we can influence how we feel by choosing what we do.

Sitting around and dwelling on things causes prolonged sadness. Doing something proactive helps you start to feel better. Plus, meditating daily helps tremendously.

When you realize you are the only thing standing between you and a smile, you become motivated to take action. The thing about feelings is you cannot sit around waiting for them to change on their own. You have to take action to change them. Meditation can help make the shift happen sooner.

Think it out.

The best way to change how you feel is to change how you think about what is bothering you. Instead of dwelling on what went wrong, identify what you learned and what you can do with that knowledge to make your next moments better.

Instead of dwelling on everything that is out of your hands, focus on things you can actually control.

How honest are you about your feelings? Do you take responsibility or blame other people for them? Do you cling to pain or let it go? You cannot avoid feelings, but you do not have to worsen them with negative thoughts.

Change the story in your head.

Sometimes when you are in a bad mood, it is tempting to cling to a story that justifies it and then retell it to yourself over and over like a picture book you've heard a million times … and then this happened … and then this also happened … and then I messed up again …

Visualize yourself closing a book and taking a new one off the shelf. Then start telling yourself a new story—one where you are a winner, one where you have power, and one where you are accepting what happened and moving on. It is clear that is a much better book to read!

Want to understand.

Even if something happened to create your bad mood, you are responsible for maintaining it, and it's easy to do that if you refuse to see the other side of situations.

If you want to believe your best friend meant to hurt you or the world is against you or your boss did not promote you because she's out to get you, that becomes your reality regardless of whether it's factual.

Instead of fueling your anger toward your friend, feel compassion for the pain she must be in: she would never hurt you on purpose. Instead of thinking the world is against you, put your day in perspective: everyone has bad days. Instead of imagining your boss is out to get you, realize she had a tough choice to make and you will have more opportunities to advance down the line.

Uplift yourself.

Disconnect yourself from negative feelings by generating positive ones. Watch something funny and silly on YouTube or something inspirational that reminds you that people are good and life is good.

I recommend validation, and every time I see it, I feel good about myself and want to pay that forward.

Use the silly voice method.

Sometimes if you swap the voice in your head with a cartoon voice, it will help take back your power from the troubling thought you allow to control you.

When you start thinking about what happened at work that went downhill, use Bugs Bunny as your mental voice. When you rehash the situation you had with your best friend, do it as one of those high-pitched mice from Cinderella. Sounds ridiculous, right? Well, it is. That is the whole point, and yet it works like magic.

Repeat.

You have tried everything, but your mind is still being stubborn. Now it is a battle of wills—the part of you that wants to let go against the part that does not.

Repeat this to yourself: "I still feel bad. I accept it. I know I will not always feel this way, and it will change as soon as I am ready, which I am now."

Simply affirm to yourself that you won't always feel bad; that you're not destined to feel angry, sad, or frustrated forever; and that you're in control of your feelings. This will motivate you to let them go.

Think of more tips for overcoming a bad mood. I bet you will be surprised to discover you have many to lean on.

Affirmation

- My thoughts and feelings change every day, moment to moment, and I control my reactions to them and change them as needed.

PATHWAY 15

Your Happiness

Life is all about taking chances, appreciating the memories,
learning from the past, and finding happiness.

—Atul Purohit

Simple Things You Can Do Today That Will Make You Happier

You know you are on the right track in life when you stop dwelling on the past and are eager to take the next step forward.

Think about that for a moment and ask yourself, What does happiness feel like?

Examine the relationship between happiness and hardship. Hardship is easy to define: It is a period of life marked by obstacles, perhaps of financial struggle or a time of personal loss. It is like the source of ongoing frustration in our lives. But happiness? What exactly is the emotion we call happiness, and why do we crave it so badly?

When trying to define happiness, it is tempting to think the I'll-know-it-when-I-see-it mindset. I have no doubt that you will, but I challenge you to dig deeper. Take just a moment right now to write down three action steps that you know will bring you happiness. Specify them.

Diana: This is what I have written down: My total happiness comes from time spent with my loved ones and on goals I know I will achieve soon. Spending quality time with my son brings me intense happiness. I also find happiness after I have read emails from long-time clients and friends who I have not heard from in the longest time.

Keep in mind, what makes me happy may not make you happy. Maybe your true happiness comes in the silence of an afternoon of meditation, or maybe you find happiness at the end of a long yet successful day. Where you find joy is not as important as long as you understand *how* you can find joy.

While working with clients, I have asked them to define the obstacles in life that are the struggles standing between them and happiness. Defining obstacles gives them clarity, and it helps chart the path to conquering them. The same holds true for happiness—in defining specific actions that drive our happiness, we learn to build those activities into our daily lives.

When we know how to get to happiness, we can be sure that we make it a regular part of our day.

Take time today to define happiness for yourself. If you have been making a habit of looking to others for what makes you happy, it is time to give that up. Doing so will make you happier almost instantly.

You may ask, "How do I know this is true?" Well, let me ask you this: Have you ever met a happy person who regularly avoids responsibility, blames and points fingers, and makes lots of excuses for his or her unsatisfying life? Neither have I. Happy people accept responsibility for how their lives unfold. They believe their own happiness is a by-product of their own thinking, beliefs, attitudes, character, and behavior.

Stop being so concerned about what others think. I may find happiness in my writing, but that does not mean you need to be a writer to be happy. Just shut out all the judgmental and well-meaning voices and only listen to yourself for a while. And do not worry if your definition of happiness seems incomplete. Embracing happiness is an ongoing process.

We have come to appreciate that happiness is much more than just an emotion; it is a path to growth and fulfillment. Overcoming daily struggles and life stresses are not easy. Action is necessary to reclaim the happiness you deserve. Action is required to realize your goals and dreams. And meditating daily can help you with the step-by-step process so you can achieve it faster.

So what choice will you make?

Affirmation

- I choose happiness rather than being concerned about what works for others.

PATHWAY 16

Starting Fresh Each Day

Each morning we are born again, what we
do today is what matters most.

—Buddha

Here Are Some Tips to Keep in Mind When Waking Up in the Morning

We may not always love everything about our lives, but deep down we do love and appreciate the magic of life itself. There is a real part of us that believes everything and anything is possible.

Sadly, though, we do not always believe these possibilities are within our reach, even when they are. The problem is we choose to believe otherwise. We choose to believe we are incapable of living our lives the way we want to—at our full potential. We choose to accept our reality as others have told us it has to be.

Wake up and smell the roses!

We do not have to do this to ourselves anymore! We have a choice. We do not have to be what others think we should be. Why not stir things up a bit and live by better rules?

It is time to take care of you—right now and every morning from here on out.

Today Can Be Great, but Only if You Allow It to Be

Why do we often feel so powerless and out of control? Because we convince ourselves that we are. We wait for things to be given to us, like entitlements. But in life, there are no true entitlements. The truth is, if you want something, you need to make it happen for yourself. You need to work hard for it. Whether today is a great day or a bad day doesn't depend on the weather. It does not depend on your mood, which is also within your control. It does not depend on anyone else. If you want to have a pleasant and productive day, then choose to have one. It is all about your perception and what you choose to believe and do.

There Is a Lot That Is in Your Control

There are plenty of things in life that are out of our control. But do not let this fool you into believing that your life as a whole is out of your control. The reality is, the life you are living is almost entirely by your own design. You have made many little choices along the way that led you down the road to where you are now. To me, saying your life is out of your control is a cop-out. It is what other people want you to believe so that they have an easier time getting you to do what they want you to do.

You Do Not Need Anyone Else's Approval

The need for approval is like an addiction. If you base all your actions on the approval of others, you ultimately find yourself running in place and sacrificing your own happiness. Do not put your happiness in someone else's hands. Learn how to say no to people and obligations that do not add value to your life. Your time on this planet is precious. As the saying goes, what you do today is important because you are exchanging a day of your life for it. Do not wait around for someone else to give you permission to live.

Complaining Is Useless Unless You Have a Solution to Replace It

Avoid being a constant complainer. It does not help you, and it certainly does not help your relationships. If you do not like your current situation, work toward changing it but do not just sit around complaining about it. Complaining will only make others nearby not want to be around you. Be someone who looks at the positive aspects of situations. And if you do find a problem that needs to be addressed, be someone who suggests a solution. The bottom line is that you will never get to where you want by complaining about where you are now. Each step in your life is preparing you for the one that comes next.

Success Is a lifestyle, Not a Result

We all want to achieve success, but we need to remember that success is not a specific achievement. Success is not crossing over some finishing line. It is the ability to fight the good fight day in and day out. Success is strength—the strength to keep pushing and to keep living your life on your own terms. Success is not an end result. It is a state of being. You do not win success. You are a success every day.

The Fact That You Have Not Given Up Is Success in Itself

It may give you little comfort to think about how you are still way deep in the struggle, but the truth is you are one of the strong people with the guts to keep going forward. Many people give up before they even begin—but not you. You wake up every day and get things done. You crawl inch by inch against the current because you refuse to give up. You refuse to accept mediocrity. You refuse to listen to others when they tell you that you are not good enough. You are still in it, fighting the good fight.

In Every Tough Situation, Kindness Must Come First

People may make ugly comments. The airline carrier may have lost your baggage. Another driver may cut you off in rush hour traffic. Or you might have lost a document that you thought you saved on your computer but didn't. These situations will continue to happen. The question is, how are you going to respond? Although your first response, like many others, will be to get upset, why not try a different approach? Anger in this kind of situation never solves problems. People are far more likely to respond positively to kindness. And you can be kind and firm at the same time. Get your point across without sacrificing your integrity. It's the only response you will not regret later.

Energy Suckers and Bullies Are Not Worth Worrying About

We sometimes allow the wrong people to take up too much space in our heads and hearts. We meet energy suckers and bullies regularly—mostly in big cities or cutthroat corporate environments. These individuals will try to get to you. They will try to influence and become a part of your life because they find their own lives to be routine and boring. They already poisoned their own lives, and now they are looking to poison yours. Do not let them!

If Someone Hurts You, Dust It Off Your Shoulders

Truth be told, if someone hurts you, chances are they have been hurt themselves. So, do your best to never take anything too personally and literally. Do not let compliments get to your head, and do not let insults get to your heart. Most people can only give others what they have received themselves. All your actions and words should come from a place of love, but not everyone will be loving in return, and that is okay. And when you do not take anything personally or literally, you liberate yourself. You can open yourself to the world freely and not have to worry about the judgments of others.

Keep in Mind, Your Focused Presence Matters

While modern technology can be life-changing in many beneficial ways, there is an aspect of this technology that greatly interferes with our lives and relationships. Do not be so addicted to a screen that you miss out on the opportunity to enjoy real life unfolding right in front of you. Give people your full and undivided attention. Do not seek mindless stimulation on a screen for no reasons, and instead, refocus on nurturing real human connections.

Good Things in Life End Too Soon When They Are Not Appreciated

This is not to say that appreciating what you have when you have it comes naturally. Our minds tend to consider the possibility that the grass on the other side is always greener. We have to learn to appreciate and love what we have. If you fall in love, do your best to nurture your love. Do not wait for things to end before you start appreciating them.

A Gentle Reminder: Today Is a Blessing

Think about how many people depart this planet every minute of every day, and you'll begin to realize that waking up in the morning is a blessing. We do not live in a world of perpetual peace, and on top of this, accidents do happen, people become severely injured, and many of them depart due to the seriousness of an injury. Getting another day to breathe, to experience life, and to do something meaningful is the greatest gift one can receive. So, make today count!

What would you add to the list? What is something positive you like to remind yourself of every day?

Affirmation

- I always choose kindness and let that guide me through my day.

PATHWAY 17

The Gift of My Intuition

Your mind will answer most questions if you
learn to relax and wait for the answer.

—William S. Burroughs

How to Hear Your Intuition When Not Knowing What to Do

Diana: Sitting in my office, I stared at the email in front of me. My heart sank as I read what was in front of me. All energy and joy left me to be replaced with confusion, anxiety, and a deep sense of frustration. As adrenaline rushed through my veins, one question overwhelmed my mind, leaving little room for the answer.

What should I do? What should I do? What should I do? I just do not know.

The email was from a client—someone I had worked with for quite a while, who was not listening to the possibilities of what life can bring, and who was causing much confusion and misery to himself and everyone around him.

And as I reread the email, I knew I had to make a decision. Could I deal with this any longer—the lack of control and sharp tone that always seemed so unnecessary, all to no improvement on his part? Did I have to stick it out? Would I tell myself to just put up with my feelings, get on with the work, and do the best I could? After all, I needed the money. Cash was tight … Could I survive without this client?

I kept repeating … What should I do? What should I do? What should I do?

And then, in that one moment, it became crystal clear. I needed to step away from the computer. I needed to get outside, and I needed to breathe. So that is exactly what I did.

Twenty-four hours later I was on the phone explaining to my client that I did not feel we were a right fit for each other any longer. We needed to bring things to an end, and it was time for us to move on … and moving on is what we did.

That day when I stepped outside and went for a walk, I found peace and quiet—a sense of calm understanding and, most importantly, a moment of absolute, pure clarity. My intuition spoke, and I listened.

I realized I had to remove myself from the situation that was causing me so much distress. Forcing myself to continue was no longer an option; it was not what my body and soul needed. Instead, I needed to follow my heart.

And so, I let go of that client and all those negative feelings, and I created space—space for new people, new places, and new experiences. And do you know what? Once I made that decision, it was like an enormous weight had been lifted from my shoulders. My energy and joy returned to me in abundance, and I knew with absolute certainty that I had made the right decision. Once again, my intuition had guided me, and she who is my heart had not let me down and never will.

Tuning into your intuition during troubled times can be difficult. With so much noise, information, and clutter within the world, our thoughts can often be clouded with distractions.

Yet there are lots of ways that you can help your intuitive voice find its way to you. Just follow these tips.

Step Away from the Situation

I have found that during these times, the best thing you can do is allow yourself some breathing space. Stand up and go for a walk, head out into the wilderness of Mother Nature, browse some antique shops, meditate for fifteen minutes, or sit with a cup of tea outside while listening to birds sing.

Whatever you love doing, whatever calms you down, now is the time to do it. Find some quiet space to let your mind wander, and your intuitive voice will have a far greater chance of being heard.

Be Honest with Yourself

It can sometimes be very easy to ignore your feelings and push them away. The fear of failure, of changing direction, and of saying no can all result in those gut feelings being pushed aside in favor of what may be perceived to be the easier option to choose.

Yet ultimately this is about your happiness, and if something does not feel right, then maybe it is time for a change. Be honest with yourself and acknowledge those unsettled feelings; they are there to guide and support you. Listening to them is a must.

Turn to Your Journal

I have found writing in a journal to be an incredible method for tuning in to my intuition. It is my safe space to release emotions, work through problems, and process my thoughts, allowing for greater self-discovery and understanding.

Next time you are having difficulty making a decision, pick up a pen and paper and let the words flow out of you. Reflect on the situation, explore those feelings, and consider the bigger picture.

This free-flowing use of personal writing can be a wonderful tool for removing blocks and letting your intuitive voice lead the way. Just let the words pour out of you. The intuitive voice is a powerful one, but it often needs a quiet, calm, reflective environment to find its way.

Learn where you can find some peace, go there when times are hard, and listen to what your heart and soul are telling you. Your intuition wants to guide and support you, so give it the space to be heard.

Learn to listen to your intuition when you have no clue on what to do next in life.

Affirmation

- I go within every day and let my intuition guide me.

PATHWAY 18

Finding the Good within the Bad

I am determined to be cheerful and happy in whatever situation I may find myself. For I have learned that the greater part of our misery or unhappiness is determined not by our circumstance but by our disposition.

—Martha Washington

Turn Tough Situations into Positive Outcomes

Diana: Most of my life, I have helped co-teach a Silva class on how to let go of stress, experience deeper happiness, and have a meaningful life. My occupation makes my occasional meltdowns all the more embarrassing. Fortunately, a meltdown I had two years ago led me to a question that completely changed how I viewed difficult situations in my life.

As I was checking in at the airport, I was told I did not have a ticket for my cross-country flight. Fortunately, I had my confirmation number with me, which I quickly gave to the lady.

"I am sorry," she said. "Although you have a confirmation number, you are not in our system. You cannot board this flight."

Suddenly, a surge of self-pity, anger, and anxiety went through my whole body. More than 150 people were expecting me in Florida the next morning to talk about how to be happier. Yet here I was fully stressed out and making this situation worse than it needed to be. I started thinking that I was not walking my talk.

I asked the ticket lady if there were any more tickets available for a cross-country flight.

"Yes," she said enthusiastically as she typed away on her keyboard.

Okay, I thought to myself, *maybe it is not going to be such a bad day after all. My day has been saved.*

She continued but then said, "If you buy the same ticket you had before, instead of $600, it will cost you $3,200."

I thought, *Oh my gosh! I was right the first time.* To me, this meant I have been totally screwed.

I needed to get to Florida as soon as possible, so I reluctantly, angrily, and self-righteously bought the ticket.

The irony of the situation did not escape me. Here I was feeling self-pity and totally stressed out while buying a ticket to help co-teach on happiness. Right away, I thought that the Universe definitely has a sense of humor.

For a long time, I have known I can choose the attitude I want and the meaning I give the events in my life. Yet there is a difference between knowing something intellectually and knowing it when things hit the roof.

Fortunately, the ticket fiasco I went through that day led me to create a simple question. I thought to myself that what I went through had a real impact in my daily life.

To make a long story short, I got to Florida on time and led a co-teaching class the next morning. That night I talked to the folks at United Airlines, and they confessed that my name was in the system but not showing up, and it was totally their fault. In fact, they decided to refund the $3,200 ticket that the company originally paid for plus my original ticket. As a matter fact, our company ended up making $600. After that, I felt like life was a bowl of cherries, and everything worked out for the best. And it seemed like I had gone through a lot of bad feelings for nothing.

But then I suddenly saw the bigger picture. I realized I often get worked up about things that frequently end up working out for the best. I wondered if there were a way to take a shortcut to this process, so I did not have to spend so much time being stressed out.

As I thought about the whole situation, I wondered what question I could ask myself that would help me face difficult situations when they occur. I did not like what I put myself through when things like that occur, so I basically ask myself, "What could be bad about this whole thing?" Because I ask that question, my brain feels obliged to give me many reasons as to why situations like that occur.

So, I wondered what it would be like to ask myself, "What could potentially be good about this?" when facing negative challenges.

In thinking back, I now realize that if I had asked this question when finding out I had no ticket, I might have come up with many good positive answers. I might have guessed it would ultimately lead to a good story or a new technique or even a refund beyond what I had imagined. And, of course, that is what ended up happening, but it would have saved me a lot of grief had I imagined that outcome while standing in the ticket line. Of course, no one knows what the outcome will be or what the future holds. Yet it seems we usually make the challenging events in our lives lead to bad feelings.

If you are going to make up things about the future, you may as well come up with a positive thought or thoughts that will empower you rather than stress you out.

For better or worse, over the next few weeks, I had plenty of opportunities to practice this simple method. For example, when my property taxes unexpectedly went up for the second year in a row, I asked myself, "What could be good about this?" That answer was easy. It could mean I added another room to the house, which means more value is added to the house for when the time comes to sell it.

And when I got sick, I asked myself, "What could potentially be good about this?" I answered, "It is helpful to have wake-up calls from time to time, as it is a reminder for me to care for my body by taking daily vitamins and not working too many hours." Though at that moment I was still feeling sick, I immediately felt better knowing that I had attached an empowering thought to the feeling of sick.

The ability to quickly create a positive thought or outcome to the events in our lives is a great aid to being happy while moving forward with the flow of life. Yet this is the exact opposite of what we do. Most of the time we create negative, disempowering thoughts whenever things seem to go wrong.

The question here, "What could potentially be good about this?" is a simple way to change how we interpret each situation in our lives. So, when you get into an argument with anyone, you can see the disagreement as a pathway to a deeper understanding of the situation rather than a doorway to anger and retaliation.

When the argument is over, you do not really know what the future holds. You might as well create a thought that empowers you. Through such empowerment, you will feel better and be more likely to act in a helpful manner.

Even up to now, I frequently ask myself, "What could be good about this?" I always come up with two or more answers, even if I do not believe in them. I find that it immediately makes me feel better and more empowered.

Instead of life feeling like a fighting battle that I needed to put up with, it feels like I have been given useful challenges that will lead me to a happy ending. It is a much better way to live than being the victim of bad news.

Affirmation

- In the worst of situations, I look for the greater good and accept what is.

PATHWAY 19

Turning Fear into Trust

The cave you fear to enter holds the treasures you seek.

—Joseph Campbell

Finding Peace after Fears

Diana: It was a hot and dry spring morning, and I started my day as usual but soon realized that my mind was entertaining fearful thoughts about my financial insecurities.

With many new ventures within the planting stage, my income flow was always shifting and unpredictable, while my financial responsibilities were consistent and guaranteed. At the time, I deemed these thoughts petty, like a parent dismissing a crying child after a fall on the playground.

What I did not realize was that my mind wanted to entertain these fear-based thoughts like a Hollywood star, and as you may know, what you focus on expands to the extreme.

Before I knew it, my body was in a state of complete anxiety and fear. I literally felt my knowledge and creativity shutting down. I felt completely powerless and a hostage to my own mind. My body felt paralyzed, and I felt disconnected from my talents and gifts of insights. I felt separate, isolated, and vulnerable. I became a victim of my fear.

In that moment, I realized the powerful impact thoughts can have on how we feel, mentally and physically. Here is what unfolded through me and the lessons I learned and treasured from this experience.

Fear is negative closed energy, referred to as inverted faith. Fear exists when we do not trust our connection to the infinite part of who we are and buy into a story about what is unfolding in our lives.

The emotions we feel are created from the thoughts we choose to focus on, consciously or unconsciously. The emotions act as markers to let us know if we are focusing on positive, empowering thoughts or fearful, limiting thoughts.

If I were to relate this to a story, it may be like a pilot believing he no longer had any guidance or support from the airport control tower in a large storm and no instruments on board to detect if he was on a collision course with another airplane. If the control tower represents the infinite part of who we are, which always knows what is best for us, it can be understandable why the pilot with no other guidance except for his own eyesight would be fearful of the situation at hand. An alarm on the plane beeping at the pilot would represent the emotions. The alarm's purpose is to get the attention of the pilot, so he can focus and realize he is off the path.

Once our emotions start to take a grip of our physical body, what can we do to move from a state of limitation and fear into an open, tranquil, peaceful, and positive state of mind?

Bring Awareness Back to the Present Moment

The first step you need to take is to bring your awareness to the present time. To do this, enter your levels of the mind by taking three deep breaths. After the air has filled your lungs, exhale through your mouth, as if you were hissing out loud.

This detoxifies your body from the heavy emotions you are experiencing and brings you back into the present moment. When I do this, I place my awareness into my feet, so I am in a feeling space within my body, rather than being in my mind and entertaining the stories that swirl around with great strength, like a dangerous storm does when ready to strike.

While being in alpha, imagine that all your emotions are in a large, slimy bucket. This breathing technique will empty the bucket, so you are empty and free from the negative thoughts that always want to take control. Please see the section titled "The Silva Centering Exercise" for more on achieving an alpha state.

Put Things into Perspective

Now that you are present, acknowledge the experience and ask yourself this question: What is the worst-case scenario that can happen to me? Once we can accept this and realize we will be okay if that happens, we are free from fear.

When I realized I had blown things out of proportion with my fears, I was able to detach from the story and put things into perspective. I like to imagine that when I am in fear, I have two wolves I can feed; one is the fearful wolf, and the other is the loving wolf. The one that gets stronger and wins is the one I feed.

Observing Your Thoughts Is Good

What has served me well in moments like this is to say, "I am not these thoughts. I am not these emotions. I am not this body. I am an infinite being having a human experience." In saying this, we immediately detach from whatever is happening and allow ourselves the choice of becoming the sufferer or the observer.

Imagine that your life has been written in a book, and the story you are living comes out from the words on the page. We can change the words of the story at any point in time to what we want them to read.

Experiences You Are Facing Can Be Changed

Before meditating, place your awareness on your heart, close your eyes, take three deep breaths, and say to yourself the following: "I am now connected to the infinite part of who I am, which already knows how to be whole and complete. I take full responsibility and accountability for this creation, I recognize how it has served me, and I am now ready to let it go. I command that the fear energy to change into unconditional love now, and this is so."

This process is incredibly empowering. We allow ourselves the opportunity to experience being our own inner masters and cocreators of our realities.

Stop Your Mind from Sabotaging You

We are constantly sabotaging our lives due to our negative ways of thinking. To prevent this, visualize a rock being thrown into a pond. Observe the ripple effect it creates when it hits the water. This is simply a distraction to your mind. It allows the process to unfold without doubt or self-sabotage. It is only our minds that can interfere with our own healing. So always keep in mind to control your way of thinking.

Be Grateful and Appreciative of All Good Things That Come Your Way

Express gratitude and appreciation for the wisdom and healing you have received.

The key to happiness is awareness. When you become aware that your mind is wandering, you can gently bring it back to the present moment. It is only in the present moment that you are empowered and can consciously choose the thoughts you engage with. The thoughts you focus on will determine where your energy flows and, as a result, is created in your life. Each thought has a vibration, which is reflected by the feeling you experience in your body.

To be able to move from a fear-based experience to an open, peaceful, positive experience, you must first take full responsibility and accountability that on some level you created the experience, and nobody else is to blame but yourself.

Just keep in mind that the choice is truly yours to make. So, do you choose to experience a fearful, limited life, or do you choose a joyful, fruitful life?

Affirmation

- I acknowledge my fearful thoughts and trust in infinite wisdom to allow them to subside.

PATHWAY 20

Befriend Your Intuition

The more you trust your intuition, the more empowered you
become, the stronger you become, and the happier you become.
—Gisele Bundchen

Your Intuition and You

Your intuition, commonly known as your gut feeling or inner guide,
is an instinct of knowing something to be true or false without any
supportive evidence. In other words, your heart just knows it is so.

Many of the great thinkers consider intuition as a major part of our
thought process and our connection to the subconscious mind. It is
the best source for tapping into our creativity and wisdom. When we
trust our intuition, it can have a great impact on our lives, allowing
us to achieve our full potential.

Trust Your Gut Instinct; it Knows It All

You know that feeling you get when something is not quite right, yet logic is telling you to do it anyway? That is your gut warning you. Chances are you have gone against your gut instinct from time to time and wished you had trusted it after the fact.

Trusting your intuition can be scarier when all the logical evidence says something to the opposite. When something does not feel quite right, it probably is not.

Make a commitment to befriend your gut feeling. The only way to learn to trust it is to take that first step. When you realize it will not let you down, you will be more willing to go with it in the future.

Always Learn to Listen

Listening to your intuition in a noisy world can often be a challenge. When you are struggling to make a decision, you have the perfect opportunity to consult your greatest teacher—your inner guide. In order to do that, though, you have to learn to listen to it.

It is important to quiet the noise around you and focus on how you feel about the question at hand. Let go of the desire to analyze, compare, and examine the issue. Just listen and pay attention to your feelings. When you are actively listening to your intuition, the answer will become clear.

Pay Close Attention

So much of the day is made up of daily routines and behaviors, including habits that bring nothing in return—behaviors that require little to no thought. If we are moving through the day using habits, then we are not allowing ourselves to tap into our intuition.

An important part of developing our intuition is paying close attention to what is happening around us. Our intuition uses information the conscious mind gathers through interaction and experience. The more information the conscious mind gathers, the more insightful our intuition becomes.

Remembering Dreams Is a Gold Mine

The subconscious mind talks to us not only through gut feelings but also through dreams. Once you begin to pay attention to your dreams, you will gain very valuable insight into your life. Recalling a dream can be hard at times, but it becomes easier when you train your brain to reflect first thing in the morning. Better yet, write them down if the dream wakes you up in the middle of the night.

You can use your dreams to help put your intuitive guide to work. Before you go to sleep, consider the challenges that are still unsolved. Spend a few minutes thinking about possible solutions. This will help trigger your inner guide to continue working while you are sleeping. Make sure you use the Silva Dream Control Technique to bring you better success when searching for a solution. Please see the section titled "The Silva Centering Exercise" for more on dream control.

Make sure you have a journal next to your bed. You might be surprised to find some creative solutions coming to you through your dreams.

Daily Meditation Is Good for You

There is no greater way to tap into your inner guide than through meditation. *Meditation* can be a scary word to many people who are not familiar with it, but there is not anything to be afraid of. Meditation is all about quieting the outside noise and excessive mental self-talk so important solutions can come through.

Start by just focusing on your breathing for a few minutes. There is no failure to meditation; it simply is what it is. The key here is to become focused on allowing your intuition to speak to you.

Start by asking for inner guidance regarding an issue you are having at the moment. Sit still and focus your mind in order to tap into the wisdom of your intuition. When you ask a specific question and are ready to receive an answer, your intuition will make it clear for you.

Developing and trusting your intuition is a skill. Start small and continue to practice it to build your intuitive muscles better and stronger. The more you choose to listen and act upon your inner guide, the better you will become at following what your gut feeling is telling you to do.

Affirmation

- Every day I pay close attention to my inner thoughts, and I let them guide me for the greater good for myself and the world.

PATHWAY 21

Dreaming Your Reality

Don't let life discourage you; everyone who
got where he is had to begin where he was.
—Richard L. Evans

Accomplishing Dreams

Diana: Follow these simple steps to find the strength to truly achieve
your passions and dreams. Even if you have different goals, these may
also work for you like they did for me.

*Mentally find a space in order to be as creative and honest as
you can.*

From the time we are little, we have been told to fit in and fit the
mold, limiting and doing away with the dreams that are embedded
deep within.

The problem is that the molds have changed as we have grown, and
it has become hard to know where our dreams end and these molds

begin. Trying to tap into your passions may be difficult, but it is definitely possible and even necessary.

Ask yourself what you would do and what you would try to accomplish if you knew you could not fail.

Pretend you are a superhero who could choose to do anything and be successful. Pretend there are no other players in the game—nobody to judge or to say you are wrong.

Just picture yourself succeeding at your dreams—whatever they may be. What would you do if you could not fail?

My list of dreams was easy to start. I knew my number-one dream immediately, which is to help people worldwide and give it 100 percent. However, after some thought, I came up with some other dreams I had not allowed myself to admit before.

Before I knew it, the list grew longer, and my heart felt even happier.

Allow yourself to write down a few options before you continue reading.

Plan out the path to your dreams.

Even when we recognize what we wish we could do and be, we believe our dreams are just dreams because they seem so far off. It may be hard to imagine them occurring in real life, but that is not the case.

What if I told you that each of your dreams is only a series of steps away from coming true, and you are only a few small tasks away from being your true self?

Take out a piece of paper. Make two columns. In the left column, write down your dreams. In the right column, next to each dream, write down one thing you can do today to achieve that dream. There is nothing enormous about this, so please follow through on your part—just one small task per dream.

Guess what. You are now on your way to achieving those dreams that seemed so far off and impossible! Reaching those dreams is just a series of small tasks.

Sometimes, the tasks I wrote down were as small as reading an article regarding research. Other times, they were more complex, like researching in depth.

Most importantly, though, they were always tasks I could tackle in one day and simple enough to avoid scaring me into procrastination.

Take good care of your most fulfilling dreams.

You have created a road map to start achievements you never thought possible or picked up where you may have left off for way too long. But let's face it—some dreams are better when they are reconsidered.

Instead of weeding out the ones that are least important, picture yourself watering the dreams that make you the happiest person in the world and help them to grow.

Success produces more success. Trust in the process, and you will get to those other dreams over time. But imagine how happy and fulfilled you will feel if you target the one that makes your heart melt.

I do my best to make myself the best life coach I can be, and it has fueled my confidence and willingness to tackle what is next.

The magic behind such a simple exercise is that you realize you can and must let your true self shine through with the power of meditation.

Just like my clients appreciate me helping them, the world will thank you for letting your true self come through in whatever projects and dreams you pursue.

Affirmation

- I focus on my dreams, old and new, and meditate on achievements I desire.

PATHWAY 22

Adjusting Your Attitude

If you don't like something, change it. If you
can't change it, change your attitude.

—Maya Angelou

Changing Your Attitude Makes a World of Difference

Sometimes changing your situation is not possible at the moment. You cannot get a new job in an instant. You cannot lose twenty pounds in one day. You cannot make someone else change against his or her will. And you certainly cannot erase the past. So what options do you have?

You can change your perception, belief, or opinion about your situation. Doing so will help you change your attitude and ultimately allow you to grow beyond the struggles you cannot control.

Here are some easy ways to start changing your perception of things while improving your attitude:

Still your mind.

In order to gain conscious control of what goes on in your mind, you need to develop a strong awareness of this process. What helps is to hold still for a moment, take a deep breath, and free your mind of all the chatter that is going on inside and all around. This makes room for a change of attitude—for something new to enter. So once in a while give yourself a break. Never say you cannot. You may have insecurities to overcome like so many, loved ones to contend with, and goals to achieve, but a break from it all is necessary. It is perfectly healthy to pause and let the world spin without you for a while. If you do not, you might burn yourself out. You must refuel on a regular basis. That means catching your breath, finding quiet time, meditating for your better good, focusing your attention inward, and making time for recovery from the confusion of your routine.

Change your focus.

From the awareness of your thoughts and emotions, you are able to consciously redirect your focus. It is time to take it willingly away from something that drags you down and focus it on something that inspires you instead. Focus on the next reasonable, meaningful step. There are no hopeless situations; there are only people who have grown hopeless about them. So, keep your hope alive through positive awareness. Do your best not to let the pain make you desperate. Do your best to not let the negativity follow you. Do your best to not let the bitterness steal your sweetness. Keep your energy moving forward. Change your thoughts, and you change your reality. Our thoughts are the makers of our moods, the inventors of our dreams, and the creators of our will. That is why we must sort through them carefully and choose to respond only to those that will help us build the lives we want.

Embrace acceptance while doing away with your worries.

Realize that, somewhere within us all, there does exist a supreme divine self who is eternally at peace. Inner peace does not depend on external conditions; it is what remains when you have surrendered your ego and worries. Peace can be found within you at any place and at any time. It is always there, patiently waiting for you to turn your attention toward it. Peace of mind arrives the moment you come to acceptance with what is on your mind. It happens when you let go of the need to be anywhere but where you are—physically and emotionally. This acceptance creates the foundation for inner harmony. The need for something to be different in this moment is nothing more than a worry, which simply leads you in circles. Remember, the same part of you that desires peace is the part of you that experiences peace. It is not complicated to achieve and is as close as your next thought.

Practicing gratitude is good.

What you must realize is that you do not really need more. You just need to appreciate what you have now. It is a beautiful and bittersweet way of thinking all at once. If you do not have what you want now, you still have enough. Be thankful for what is, and also be thankful for what is yet to come, for that only means there are still many possibilities available to reach. Find peace in the thought that you cannot ever have it all or even know it all. You are always just a fraction of the whole. For if you were not, there would be nothing more to experience. Value what you know and also value the countless things you do not yet understand but will in due time. Life will always be incomplete and a bit unbalanced. Realize this and embrace it. Be happy and sad at the same time, hungry and thankful, nervous and excited—and be okay with that.

Consider your struggles as growing pains.

Remind yourself that there is hardly any happiness, passion, or success without struggle. If the path is easy, you are likely going the wrong way. Everything that happens helps you grow, even if it is hard to see it right now. Circumstances will direct you, correct you, and perfect you over time. Sometimes these circumstances knock you down—*hard.* There will be times when it seems like everything that could possibly go wrong, is. And you might feel like you will be stuck in this rut forever … but you know better. When you feel like quitting, remember that sometimes things have to go very wrong before they can be right. Sometimes you have to go through the worst to arrive at your best. Our most significant opportunities are often found in times of great difficulty. Sometimes you will face your greatest struggles when you are closest to your biggest miracle.

An ending always starts a new beginning.

Everything in life has to come to an end at some time or another. It is important to acknowledge and accept the end of circumstances—to walk away when something has reached its conclusion. Closing the door, turning the page, moving on, and so on—it does not matter what you call it; what matters is that you leave the past where it belongs, so you can enjoy the life that lies ahead. This ending is not the end; it is just your life beginning again in a new way. It is a page in your story where one chapter fades into the next.

When all else fails, use your body.

The mind is reflected in your body by responding to its levels of tension—such as by how fast or slow you are breathing, as well as the speed of movement and mental focus. Likewise, your body mirrors your thoughts, feelings, and mood and responds to your state of mind as well as the questions you ask and the words you speak. Therefore, if the mind and body are constantly connected, one has a direct effect on the other. It becomes clear that if we directly and consciously take control of one, it will influence and transform the other. So, by mindfully adjusting how you use your body, you can directly influence your state of mind and dramatically transform your attitude.

For example, imagine you are in a bad mood. Your shoulders are hanging down forward, your breathing is shallow, and you are frowning. Go ahead and do this right now—experience how it influences your state of mind. Then, do the opposite: stand up straight and put a big smile on your face. Take some deep, strong breaths and stretch your arms into the air. Don't you feel better?

The bottom line here is to take the temple your Creator has given you and use it wisely. Your body is the best tool for changing your attitude in an instant.

The mind is your battleground. It is the place where the greatest conflict resides, and more than half of the things you thought were going to happen never do. But if you allow those thoughts to dwell in your mind, they will succeed in robbing you of peace, joy, and, ultimately, your life. You will think yourself into a nervous breakdown, into depression, and into defeat. I know because I have been there before many times.

To be honest, there is so much about your fate that you cannot control. It makes no sense to neglect all the things that you can control. You can decide how you spend your time, with whom you socialize, and with whom you share your life, money, and energy. You can pick your words and the tone of voice in which you speak to others. You can choose what you will eat, read, and learn every day. You can choose how you are going to respond to unfortunate situations when they arise and whether you will see them as a conflict or opportunities for growth. And most importantly, you can choose your attitude, which dictates pretty much everything else.

What helps you change your attitude from negative to positive when life gets stressful and painful?

Affirmation

- I improve my attitude by always controlling my reactions to situations—especially ones that I have no control over.

PATHWAY 23

Justice and Fairness—It Is Not as Bad as It Seems

You're going to go through tough times - that's life.
But I say, 'Nothing happens to you, it happens for
you.' See the positive in negative events.

—Joel Osteen

Bypassing through Tough Situations Quickly

Everything may seem to be going smoothly, and then, suddenly, unforeseen things happen in life. Someone steals your wallet, someone you loved left you, or maybe your health declined.

It is not fair. You did not see it coming or plan for it. You have so many feelings and frustrations, and you do not know what to do first—or if you want to do anything at all.

It would be so much easier to sit around feeling bad, look for people to blame and complain to, or rehash what you could have done to make things different. You may even think about what other people should have done to help you.

These are all great options if you want to maximize your misery and feel justified in doing so. But they're not the best choice if you want to move on. You have to do this eventually when something bad happens, and the faster you do it, the sooner you will improve your situation.

There are plenty of opportunities to practice dealing with kindness and wellness. If you would like to work on improving your life and how you respond, you may find these tips helpful.

Acceptance needs to be a priority in life.

Dealing with a bad situation can be a lot like dealing with grief, and people often go through the same stages. First, there is shock and denial, pain and guilt, anger and agreement, and the list goes on. You might not be able to fully express your emotions, but you can decide to accept what has happened, regardless of how you feel about it. The sooner you accept it, the sooner you can act from where you are, which is the only way to change how you feel.

It is like the saying goes: When you do not feel ready, do not wait for your feelings to change to take action. Take the action, and your feelings will change.

Eliminate the word fair *as much as you can.*

As kids, we are all about fair. For example, "He took my ball—that's not fair," "You said you would buy me a new tricycle—that is not fair," I had that crayon first—that is not fair," and so on.

You would think we would learn early in life that it is not always going to be fair, but instead, we cling to how we think things should be. Hard work should be rewarded. Kindness should be reciprocated.

When things do not work out that way, we feel angry at the world and bad for ourselves. Feeling angry about life's injustices will not change the fact that things are often unexpected and beyond your control. When you start going on an unfair spiral, remind yourself that it is what it is and then choose a reaction that aligns with the way you would like the world to be.

Focus on life lessons.

Diana: I remember years ago my best friend recommended that I pretend everyone was enlightened but me and that everyone I met was here to teach me something positive. She said she read those words somewhere, but she was not sure where. Her words have stayed with me ever since.

In this way, you will see that someone who annoys or frustrates you also provides an opportunity to work on your patience. This same mindset can help improve the way you interpret and respond to events in your life.

If you lost your job, perhaps the life lesson is to determine your true purpose. If your relationship falls apart, the life lesson may be to become more independent. Focusing on the lesson allows you to work on positive change, which will make you feel empowered instead of defeated.

Question your problems.

We often turn minor upsets into huge failures in our minds. Yet some things are challenging, such as losing your job, car, or—worse yet—someone you love. But most situations can be resolved.

Sometimes they are blessings in disguise. I remember reading an interview in which it was stated that one hundred people were interviewed who had near-death experiences. The majority of the subjects experienced spiritual awakenings, proving that what did not kill them only made them stronger.

Whatever you are dealing with, as bad as it may feel, is it really the end of the world? And most importantly, if you bounced back with an even better situation, a higher paying job, or a more satisfying relationship, how impressed would you be with yourself? Think about that.

Make "get strong" your affirmation.

This idea has saved me many times throughout my life. At the age of sixteen, I spent four weeks hospitalized with an illness that caused me to miss out on a lot in life. So much seemed unfair about how it all panned out.

Then, suddenly, I remembered what my best friend told me: "I know you feel powerless right now, but you are going to shake the world when you get stronger." Whenever I deal with any kind of adversity, I remind myself to keep strong.

Changing the path of life makes you stronger.

It is easy to become attached to the path you are on, and this is even more true if it makes you happy. When something or someone throws you off beat, you may feel disconnected from who you want to be or what you want to do in life.

It may help to remember that a hurdle does not have to destroy your plans, for it is just a hurdle. Even if you lose your job, you can still pursue your professional goals—and maybe even more efficiently.

There is always more than one way to turn things around for the better. The sooner you focus on finding a new way, the sooner you will turn a bad thing good.

Ask yourself how someone you respect and look up to would handle the situation.

I recently put my whole heart into a quote-of-the-day competition. And, of course, I had to get votes to win. Well, what can I say ... I ended up in third place.

When I did not win first place, I felt disappointed and even a little embarrassed. I felt like I had failed in front of lots of people. To me, my best was not good enough.

So, I asked myself how someone with integrity would handle the situation. The organizer of the event congratulated the winner, and the winner said it hadn't been easy. What I needed to do first was identify everything I learned from the experience and move on to the next goal with my head held high. Acting on that advice made me feel proud of myself instead of disappointed.

People will remember the things you accomplish, but the way you handle life's challenges can affect them just as strongly. Life happens, and it is not always easy. You can cry over it and fight it or see dealing with life's challenges as the most important challenge of all.

You cannot always get what you want, but you can work at being who you want to be no matter what life throws at you. Therefore, learn to be the best you can be.

Affirmation

- I have the ability to get past every situation I encounter that seems unfair because I am strong.

PATHWAY 24

Seeing Things Clearer

Once you replace negative thoughts with positive
ones, you'll start having positive ones.

—Willie Nelson

Eliminating Negative Thought Patterns

A big part of our negative thoughts is our self-judgment. In order to become more positive in our thoughts, we must begin by accepting who we are and stop judging ourselves.

Wishing we were skinnier, happier, in a better job, or living in a different house or country is really a waste of energy. Time could be spent working on what we want to improve, so we can be happier with who we are.

The only way to be the person you want to be is to accept who you are and take action daily to support your growth.

Below you will find how to eliminate negative thought patterns and get your mind back on track.

Question every negative thought that comes to mind.

A thought is our way of talking to ourselves. Because our thoughts influence our lives, it is extremely important to shape our thoughts, so they are positive, encouraging, and motivational, which keeps us moving forward.

By questioning your negative thoughts, you are looking for evidence of the truth. If they are true, then you can begin to train your mind to stay positive. Yet, more than likely, they are false, and it is when you prove to yourself that they are not real that you can begin to let them go and move on.

Talk to yourself.

When supportive friends surround you, you will often hear things like "I know you can do it" or "It is awesome that you are doing well." But when you talk to yourself, you may hear things like "I am not sure about this," "I hope I can stay well," "What am I doing?" or "Who am I fooling?"

Listen to what you are telling yourself. Your subconscious does not know the difference between a serious thought and a boasting thought.

Eventually, after hearing the same kind of statements over and over, you begin to believe in them. This kind of self-talk, even if it is not real in your mind, will result in decreased self-confidence and add to a negative self-image.

If you are not cheering yourself on, then how can you expect others to support you? Create a few affirmations about yourself and start your morning by looking yourself in the mirror while carrying on a good conversation with yourself. It is amazing how saying a few kind words to yourself will change your outlook on the day.

Approval only comes from you.

Our need for approval plays an important role in our thoughts. It destroys our ability to think positively and prevents us from our journeys. Instead, we think and act based on other people's ways of life.

The need for approval is negatively affecting our lives. We procrastinate, avoid doing important things, feel anxious and fearful, and become stuck in worry—all in the quest to gain approval.

Make the decision to stop seeking approval and trying to be someone you are not. Stop feeling the pressure to do something you do not believe is right for you. Stop doing things with the influence of someone else's way of life and, finally, stop hiding how you feel.

Always think big.

It is a common thing to underestimate ourselves by setting small goals. In other words, we limit our bets on success by setting goals that are attainable. This kind of mindset is more harmful than helpful.

Pushing ourselves to test our strength and abilities allows us to continue to grow. The world has infinite resources available, and when you think big, you begin to tap into the possibilities.

Thinking big means thinking beyond what you can see, setting extremely high standards and looking at challenges in terms of opportunities instead of barriers and fears. Thinking big means knowing anything and everything is possible to change for the better.

You are a work in progress.

Start accepting the fact that you and your life are a work in progress. Face it: You will never be at a place when everything is the way you want it to be. That is just the way life is.

Think about it. What if everything were to be perfect? Would it not be a bit boring?

Sure, it might be amazing for a while, but how would you feel if you had nothing to dream about or no goals to achieve? Just because you are a work in progress does not mean you are not good enough today. It does not mean your life is any less meaningful because it is not perfect.

Being a work in progress means you have hopes and dreams and want to do better tomorrow. If you recognize life as a work in progress, it makes it easier to accept life as it is today, knowing something better is out there waiting to be noticed.

The big plus here is that you are in control. You can choose to be positive, or you can accept the situation the way it is. And honestly, it is easier to stay in a negative mindset than to do the work necessary to move back into a positive space. Just know that it gets easier with practice, and the rewards are more than worth the effort. So, meditate to make it all easier and possible to achieve.

What are you going to do today to change for the better? What part of your life needs changing?

Affirmation

- I work on seeing things differently, and I am open to change.

Sticking with Goals When the Going Gets Tough

Imagine with all your mind. Believe with all
your heart. Achieve with all your might.

—Unknown

Your Goals and Dreams

We all face obstacles in pursuing our goals, whether it be professional or personal.

We think we are on the right track, but then we realize we have chosen the wrong approach. We are passionate and hard-working, but our support systems disconnect when we need them the most—like making progress when we run out of time, money, or resources.

Tough as we may be, we all have our breaking points when the potential rewards stop justifying the effort—usually at the point that separates your best shot and your best reality.

Before you throw in the towel and go back to something safe, ask yourself the following questions:

Why did you originally pursue this goal, and has anything changed for the better?

You had reasons for committing yourself to this plan. Maybe you visualized a financially free future once you start a new job, or you realized that if you lose some weight, you would live longer and healthier.

Chances are, you still want those things as much as you did before; you just stopped believing you could have them because your attempts have yet to produce results. Ask yourself, if you push through the discomfort, will it be worth it in the end?

Can too much information hold you back?

With so much information at your fingertips, it is easy to overwhelm yourself with more knowledge than you can utilize. You read inspirational quotes, participate in teleconferences and workshops, read up on how to do this and how to do that, and join blogs to communicate with others about the outcome.

One of two things happen as a result: (1) You spend more time planning what you want to do instead of taking action, or (2) you devote minimal energy to multiple projects instead of committing to one solid approach. Instead of overflowing in all that information you are reading, why not narrow it down and start again from a less overwhelming space?

Set goals that are specific, achievable, measurable, and realistic and target a date.

Being specific is knowing exactly what your world will look like when you achieve this goal. Being measurable is having a specific plan to mark your progress as you go. Being attainable is having the attitude and power to make your goal a reality. Being realistic means you're are willing and able to do the required work, while setting a target date makes a concrete time frame for completion to create a sense of urgency.

Diana: I learned this method through my best friend. If you did not set your goals with these specifics in mind, you might have set yourself up to a journey of growth that goes in circles. How can you possibly make something happen if you do not know exactly what you want or did not really believe you could achieve it? Are you really willing to walk away when you did not give yourself every opportunity to succeed? No, of course not!

What if the goal is not reached?

Oftentimes, I stop moving forward because I'm afraid of failure. I may fear that others will be disappointed in me or judge me. In reality, no one ever judges us like we judge ourselves, and we always grow and learn through the process of striving, regardless of what we attain.

If you do not keep moving forward, you will never know how far you could have gone and you will miss out on being the person you can become through the effort itself. Like the saying goes, shoot for the moon, for even if you miss, you will land among the stars.

Are you fearful of success?

One of my biggest problems is that I do not like responsibilities. There are many things I would have liked to do, but I hold myself back because I do not want the power to impact, hurt, or disappoint other people. That does not mean I don't have dreams. It is just that I am scared of what achieving them will involve.

If you can relate to this feeling, perhaps you will respond well to the affirmation I have been repeating: great power comes with great responsibilities, but it also brings great rewards. If you play it safe, you will not hurt or disappoint anyone, but you also will not help or inspire anyone. Equally as important, you will not be able to help yourself, much less inspire yourself.

Are you thinking things through?

Sometimes our emotions give us ideas about what we want and what we should do, but other times they are just responses to stress, and maybe even indications that we are on the right track. If you act in that moment of intense emotion—be it fear, anger, or frustration— you may regret it once the situation has passed.

Sit back, close your eyes, take a deep breath, and relax from head to toe. Take notice of what you are feeling—feeling it fully, without judgement. Then mentally take action in the mind as to what you need to do and when it has to be done. Search for a sign, answer, or solution. At least then you will know you made your decision in a moment of peace and clarity.

Be honest about why you gave up.

We need to be honest all around! Would you really tell your loved ones, "I stopped trying to lose weight because eating junk food is more important to me than having many more years to spend with you"? No!

Or would you tell your mother, "I decided not to go to school because I would rather spend all my time with my boyfriend of three months than prepare for my future that will ensure me that I will not end up jobless or homeless"? No!

If you lay it out like above, odds are you will realize you had a really good reason for doing what you did, and no matter how challenging the process is, it is worth pushing ahead while practicing daily what you have learned from the Silva Method techniques and tools.

Would life be better without goals?

This may not sound motivational, but sometimes giving up is actually a good thing. Perhaps you set a completely unrealistic goal, and pursuing it is causing doubts and anxiety. Or maybe the goal is not in your best interest or the best interest of your loved ones, and it is better to get out.

You could easily use this as a justification to escape from the situation, so think about it carefully. Is this goal really a good one when you weigh all the pros and cons of its achievement?

What would you tell a friend?

Would you tell your best friend to throw in the towel because she cannot possibly reach her goal? Or would you give her your finest motivational speech and help her see what you see in her potential? Unless you are her worst enemy who hopes that she fails in life, odds are you would push her to be her best—so why not push yourself?

It may sound silly, but you need to be your own best friend. You, more than anyone in this world, deserve your belief and motivation.

If you have gone through all these questions and still feel determined about the decision to give up, you have my blessings to let go of that goal.

But your lingering doubts may turn into negative self-talk. Keep working toward the dreams that fill you with so much passion.

Or take a different approach. Whatever you do, do not give yourself a reason to one day say the words "I quit because I was scared."

What would you do if you were facing situations like this?

Affirmations

- I give my all to my goals for the greater good for all, including myself.
- Before I decide to end a goal, I ask myself if it is because I may be afraid.

PATHWAY 26

Taking Chances / Overcoming Fears

Life begins at the end of your comfort zone.

—Neale Donald Walsh

Stepping Out of Your Comfort Zone

Diana: For as long as I can recall, I have been somewhat of an eager person. My grandfather died when I was a child, and some of my earliest memories consist of panic attacks whenever I found myself alone. In my mind, I thought I had to keep my loved ones in sight at all times, so there would be no chance of them disappearing on me as my grandfather did.

From that point on, I slowly began to overcome my fears of separation from my family because new anxieties took its place. Whether I was nervous about meeting new people or panicking over unexpected change, the anxiety I was in was all-consuming and endless.

Somewhere in my later teenage years, my best friend suggested that I start exercising to relieve some stress instead of meditating. The first day at the recreational center was a source of anxiety in itself. Between checking in, finding an open machine, and deciding what to do next, the entire process was mentally overwhelming and exhausting.

For a while, I was too nervous to step foot in the recreational center without my best friend being there with me because I was scared to be left alone with my thoughts for too long.

Separation from familiar people is a scary thing in a time when you are constantly connected no matter where you are. You can be standing on a mountaintop all alone, but with thousands loved ones in your mind. And with this being the new reality, any amount of time to yourself can be a source of anxiety.

Eventually, I learned that being alone at times is a good thing. Each day I would step outside of my comfort zone and do something new. Some days it would be a walk around the block with only my silence. Other days, it was going to a yoga class by myself.

Some of my challenges were harder than others. I now find that taking yoga classes allows me to ease into workouts on my own.

Although some days were successful, other days I would have serious setbacks. The worst of these was quitting my yoga classes or workouts because I was embarrassed to complete my workout with a specific person being there.

After years of being teased for my lack of coordination, I feared judgment and began to feel that all eyes were on me with every move I made.

Then, suddenly, I had a huge realization that only I can make myself happy. Stressing over a situation will not change it, and being self-conscious in the yoga class will definitely not get me in shape. This understanding pushed me to keep going forward, though it did not resolve my fears. In the beginning, I would still worry about what others thought and spend time stressing over every situation that was slightly outside of my comfort zone.

Even though I realized I had to make a change, I also realized I would not be able to do it overnight. Small steps on a daily basis gradually allowed me to be more comfortable with myself, both in the yoga class and out. I slowly became more confident and frequently engaged in more situations than I ever imagined.

In the beginning, my exercise was meant to relieve stress, but it only ended up causing me more stress. I think this is because I was not doing it for the right reasons. I thought exercise would be a cure-it-all that would wipe away my problems with only a few visits to yoga classes. In due time, I began to see exercise for its greater meaning. It could be a short-term reliever for anxiety, but it was a lifelong journey toward better health. As soon as I started to see it that way, my fear reduced automatically.

This way of life required me to be a little better each and every day and to be stronger mentally and physically than I have ever been before.

Many people think of exercise as a way to strengthen your body and calm your mind. But I realized that was not what I needed. I needed to strengthen both my body and mind, and I had to do so by challenging both. I could have easily gotten in shape at home as many others do, but that would not have challenged my anxious mind. I would have felt safe and calm in my comfort zone.

The best thing I ever did was to get that yoga membership and force myself to get there. It not only led me to a love for physical activity, but it also led me to a feeling of confidence that I had never felt before.

Anxiety is a tough thing to deal with. It makes you feel guilty and scared, and it can keep you from doing things you love in life.

While anxiety never truly went away, it no longer controls or defines me. The best way to reduce the impact it has on you is to do your best to step outside of your comfort zone whenever you can. Even though it feels frightening at first, doing a little more each day can help make it seem less overwhelming. And in due time, you will be able to do things you never knew were possible. Time and effort will make your journey easier, which will lessen the burden of your struggle.

For me, making the active decision to push myself is what got me through the worst of my anxieties. Now, when anxiety does its best to challenge me, I know that I am stronger than before; therefore, I am the stronger one.

Affirmations

- Even if something scares me, I take a chance to see if it would be for my benefit.
- If I don't at least try, I'll never know what could have been.

PATHWAY 27

Facing and Moving Forward

Remember you can't reach what's in front of you,
until you let go of what's behind you.

—Buddha

Letting Go

Let's face it. Once in a while, we all dwell on the past, and that is okay. We are human beings with emotions. As we live life and experience it to its fullest, it is only natural that we sometimes cling to what once was. But when our desire to cling to the past affects our future, we begin an unhealthy and obviously endless battle with ties that can hold us back from achieving our goals.

Diana: For the past two years, I have dreaded spring. Though many people would embrace the rain, the newborn green, and the post-winter reawakening, I would plead for spring to pass. For me, spring is a hard reminder of a series of unfortunate events.

Just this past year I experienced three losses that made me think I had to be miserable because one of them was the loss of a dear family member. I carried this burden with me, letting it hold me back, which made certain dates, locations, and possibilities off limits. I dreaded every time it was spring because my emotions would spin out of control, and I was scared to face reality. Sometimes they did, but it took me awhile to realize that it was me allowing my emotions to surface.

Whether you have experienced a tragic death, a breakup, or a burst of bad luck, certain people, places, and things hold you in the past.

Maybe these tips can help you let go of them and move forward with life. Keep in mind that you must meditate daily in order to bypass whatever you're holding on to that belongs in the past.

Ground yourself to Mother Earth.

Allow yourself time to hold on to what is holding you to your past. Though this may seem like a strange piece of advice, this is the first step in the process of moving on forward.

For example, set aside thirty minutes every night to think of the past and then challenge yourself not to do that before or after then. Little by little, you will allow the past to be in the past while moving forward with your future. Remember to keep the lesson as a reminder but never allow the past to be in your present moment or in your future at all.

Think it through clearly.

When you begin to dwell on the past more than you feel is healthy, ask yourself a series of open-ended questions:

- Why does this memory matter to me?
- Does it serve me to modify certain opportunities because they remind me of this memory?
- What is the worst that can happen if I am faced with the ugly reminder of this memory?

- What can I do to live with this memory, accept it, and move forward?
- And does it really hold back? Does that really hold truth?

And, of course, omit the words *could, should,* and *would* from your vocabulary. They will only cause confusion, especially when you already know what must be done.

Stop mentally rehashing things repeatedly.

In one of my recent emails, I mentioned that people love to relive their problems mentally in hopes of gaining new insight or hearing what we want to hear. I can guarantee you that this will not work. In fact, you may be even more inclined to think of the past.

If you stop telling your story, you will realize each day that you are the one in control. You have the power to let go of whatever is holding you to your past.

Throw them in a box once and for all.

This is a simple way of letting go of your past. Find any small box and stuff it with memories you may have of whatever is holding you back. For me, it was a few letters, a bracelet, a picture, and a heart.

Put everything in the box and hide it until you are ready to revisit it again with a different mindset. The key is to not allow yourself to hide it forever but to get yourself to a place where you can achieve acceptance.

Put it into words as soon as you can.

You do not have to be an author to get your feelings on paper. All you have to do is take a pen and write down everything you have ever wanted to tell yourself, or if it is a situation, personify the memory.

A piece of paper is tougher than you think, so do not hold anything back. Now comes the hardest part: get rid of your letter. Bury it, shred it, or even burn it. Whatever brings you peace, do it. I thought this was silly advice until I tried it myself. It really felt wonderful and liberating.

Realize who matters.

Take the words of Dr. Seuss to heart: "Those who mind don't matter and those who matter don't mind." Take this advice as an opportunity to discover who is really touching your life now. Who is truly there for you? And think on how you can enjoy your shared connection with a person in your life while doing your best to forget about who else was once there for you.

Reciprocate the effort.

It is like the saying goes. What goes around, comes around, so be there for those who are there for you. This is a great step in building new and meaningful relationships to help focus on the present.

Perhaps they are held down too. You can help each other. This is why reciprocated relationships are the only ones that truly work and last.

Find what works best for you.

Whatever is holding you down does not own you. It cannot dictate your actions, make you feel inferior, or restrict you from living the life you want without your consent. You are your own person—every expression and emotional part of you.

Find something fun and unique, make it your own, and grow from that. For me, rediscovering my hobbies and contributing to the Silva Method in doing humanitarian acts has helped me tremendously.

Disconnect the negative and reconnect the positive.

By disconnecting from whatever is holding you back, you are reconnecting with yourself—the person within. Open up that anchor box you have kept hidden. Look at its contents with acceptance, not pessimism or a self-defeating attitude.

Walk the streets you once walked, and maybe you will notice a new store that opened, or you might get a chance to see something beautiful that you never thought of along the way.

Make new, positive memories.

Keep yourself busy with physical activity. Join a community club or a yoga class and hang around with like-minded people. Meet someone who has no clue what you do for a living and why you do it and just live to the fullest as much as you can while having fun with life itself. Every day you have the opportunity to make new memories happen. This is a gift we often take for granted, and we shouldn't.

So remember, nothing has to ever hold you down to your past or anything else. If you choose to let go, they will become slight road bends in the endless journey of life.

Affirmation

- I allow nothing to hold me back.

PATHWAY 28

Good, Better, Best!

Don't be afraid to give up the good and go for the great.

—Steve Prefontaine

When Fear and Confusion Hold You Back from Improving

Diana: Have you ever had an inner knowing that it was time to make life changes, but you felt too confused and scared to make the change?

I have certainly felt that way many times in my life. After I graduated from college years ago, I felt completely confused about what I was going to do with my life. I would ask myself questions: How am I going to find meaning in life? What should I do for a career? How can I make my dreams and goals a reality?

But what if you feel so confused about your life that you end up doing nothing?

I remember one cloudy night lying in bed reading fiction books for hours. I love and enjoy reading. I wanted to escape from the nonstop confusion and endless, pointless questions running through my mind. The reality is I was scared of what my future would come to be. I was scared to start a job but scared not to. I was scared to move away from the comforts of home, but deep down I could not wait to get out and be on my own. I was scared of the unknown but also excited by the fact that anything good and positive could happen.

I was afraid to make a change, so I tricked myself into thinking that it was too complicated and confusing. For a couple of months, I did nothing, and my frustrations grew as days and months passed.

It is a fear that grips you with confusion when you have an inner knowing that things are off or you want to make a major life change, but you feel too confused to take action. That can also be related to fear-based confusion.

It seems like there are too many problems, unknowns, reasons, ifs, ands, buts, why nots, or decisions that are difficult to make. So, staying confused would be easier to deal with.

Does this sound familiar to you? Maybe you are confused about making a career change, moving to a new city, ending a relationship, or getting your finances back in order. I think we have all experienced this kind of fear that grips us with confusion in one form or another, and I know how frustrating it can be.

What I have noticed is that the awareness of fear as the base for your confusion can drastically reduce your stress about it.

You are certainly not alone or helpless, for that matter. And luckily, fear that grips us with confusion is easy to move beyond.

Below are some ways to move through life confusion and finally become clear on what you want so you can take action toward it.

Always follow your passion and what brings excitement to your life.

If the fear runs deep, following your excitement will help. For example, instead of trying to answer the question, "What should I do with my life?" ask yourself, "What excites me right now?"

Make a list of all the activities and experiences that excite you, but do your best to not judge your list, much less yourself.

For me, simply walking to a local cafe for a smoothie each morning is something that really excites me. I can hardly wait to get there. Keep in mind that it does not matter if things on your list seem small or insignificant. What matters is the thought that it excites you.

There are several benefits to following what excites you in this moment. First, you start to feel more excited about your life, and second, your excitement usually leads you to people and experiences that will help you set a direction for yourself.

Follow what excites you at the moment and know that your sources and intuition from time to time are going to improve, shift, and change for the better as you grow. Following your excitement is much less discouraging than trying to figure out your whole life. In addition, it leaves room for growth and gives you the freedom to continually try new things.

Decide what direction you will take.

Decide very clearly on the direction you want to go. Making a clear decision is the quickest way out of confusion. I know this sounds obvious, but sometimes we have silly inner thoughts that hold us back. Thoughts like, *I am not good enough, I do not deserve this,* or *I am never lucky.*

But you most definitely are good enough, and you so do deserve peace and all that comes with life no matter what you are telling yourself. Believe in yourself enough to make a decision and know that you will make the right choice. Desire what you want with all your heart and expect it to take place. Don't worry about making a bad decision because there is no such thing as a bad decision. In my opinion, making no decision at all is often the worse decision to make.

In the example above, after a couple of months of sinking deeper into my confusion, I decided to pack a couple of things and take a hiking trip with my friends. I did not really have any idea how that was going to help me answer my big life questions, but it excited me anyway. When I got back home from that trip, I felt confident and even more excited about life. Then I made a solid decision about my future, and that completely changed everything for me.

The point here is it did not really matter what I did. It was my decision to do something that got me out of my confusion.

Once you make the initial decision, the universe will start to provide you with people and experiences that help you move forward. So breathe, become aware of how your decision feels in your body, and act on whatever feels good and pure to you.

Let go of all your expectations.

Expectations usually lead to disappointments. That happens when we finally make the decision to change and proceed to come up with a detailed plan for how it should all go down. We immediately search for something that will make us feel secure in the face of change.

But the truth is you can manifest much quicker when you open yourself up to all the possibilities that you have not yet thought through. It is perfectly okay to focus on what you want. Simply focus on what excites you and the capability of doing it right now. This allows you to feel joy in the moment instead of making your joy dependent on a certain outcome in the future.

You are meant to be here at the now. As you focus on following what excites you in this moment, the fuzziness of confusion begins to clear, and you can see in what direction you are heading. Then, moving toward things with inner confidence becomes natural.

Know that it is okay to feel unsafe in the process, but I also know from experience that the vulnerability associated with change is completely worth it. You are worth more than you can imagine. Do not let the confusion hold you back more than it has already. Once you take the first step, everything else will unfold for you in a blink of an eye.

Therefore, why not take the first step toward a better life so that you can live to the best of your ability.

Affirmation

- Good is good, better is even better, but best is the best! I don't stop until I have, feel, and am the best.

Changing Your Thoughts to Improve Your Circumstances

You must learn a new way to think before
you can master a new way to be.
—Marianne Williamson

Changing Your Way of Thinking for the Better

Diana: As the saying goes, she who teaches others teaches herself. This holds true in life, not only because constant repetition helps impress facts without a doubt of the mind but also because the process of teaching gives greater insight into the subject taught. This is one of the reasons why I take on new coaching clients, write about new developments, and share them with you even when my lifestyle is full. I believe in sharing the strategies that have taught me positive growth.

One of the strategies I teach repeatedly is self-examination, which is basically the art of asking ourselves the right questions. Why is this strategy so important? Because the questions we ask ourselves become thoughts. Thoughts then become words. Words then become actions. Actions then become character, and character changes everything.

Truth be told, when times get tough and big problems start to appear, as they often do, it is the strength of who we are that sees us through. This is our character.

And because our character is directly influenced by what we say, think, and do on a daily basis, I want you to think about how you have been speaking to yourself lately. Have you been using empowering, encouraging words you would say to a friend? Or are you using belittling remarks you would shout to an enemy? Are the negative remarks about life things you might say if you had no faith and hope?

All day long you speak silently to yourself, and a part of you believes every word you say. Therefore, it is so important to stay mindful when problems arise.

Questions to Keep in Mind

If you really wanted to be positive and happy right now, what would it take?

Your greatest weapon against stress and negativity is your ability to choose one thought over another. Happiness escapes from those who refuse to see the good in what they have. When life gives you every reason to be negative, that is when you need to think, walk, and be positive as much as you can.

What are you thankful about right now?

Smile not because life has been easy, perfect, or exactly as you had assumed it to be but because you choose to be happy and thankful for all the good things you have and all the problems you know you don't have. Always be thankful and grateful for being alive.

What words do you need to omit from your thoughts and vocabulary?

Stop disgracing yourself for everything you are not and start giving yourself credit for everything you are. We have to be our own best friend, not our own worst enemy. Self-pity will only feed the negative feelings you want to get rid of.

What are you holding on to that you need to let go of?

One of the hardest lessons in life is letting go of what is not working for you any longer, be it guilt, anger, love, or loss. Change is never easy, and it never will be. You fight to hold on, and you fight to let go. Most of the time, letting go is the healthiest way forward, as it clears out toxic negative thoughts from the past. You emotionally release yourself from the things that once meant a lot to you, so you can move beyond the past and the pain that comes with it. Again, it takes hard work to let go and refocus your thoughts, but it is worth it in the long run.

Should you wallow in what is not working or create an action plan to help you move forward on your own?

Imagine how much more effective and happier you would be if, instead of denying, blaming, dreading, and fighting against certain situations and tasks, you simply handled them. Meditating can help you calm the mind, which stops the negative thoughts and allows you to find a solution in order to achieve your outcome much easier.

Can you respond from a place of clarity and strength rather than in a negative frame of mind?

Every time you are tempted to react in the same, old-fashioned way, ask yourself if you would rather be a prisoner of your past or a creator of your future. Always keep in mind that our character is often most evident in our highs and lows. Be humble when achieving goals, be strong when mastering it one by one, and be faithful in between, for it is all good.

How can you be of help to everyone when help is needed?

Life is a gift, and it offers us the chance, opportunity, and responsibility to give something back by becoming more. The best way to find yourself when times are tough is to give yourself in the service of a cause greater than yourself. It is like when we keep reminding our Silva Graduates about meditating. Always keep in mind to include someone other than yourself in order to make a positive shift in this world for the better.

Are your expectations too high, and are they hurting or helping you?

Expectations are like cold ice. The longer you hold them, the faster they melt. Life becomes easier when you lower your expectations. Therefore, let go a little and appreciate your life and relationships for what they are. When you do, life will change for the better right before your eyes.

Who, or what, needs your forgiveness?

Forgiveness does not always lead to healing relationships and situations. Some relationships and situations are not meant to be healed. Forgive anyway, and let what is meant to be, be—and set yourself free. When you hold resentment toward another, you are connected to that person or condition by an emotional link that is stronger than life itself. Forgiveness is the only way to dissolve that link and break free. If you have not done this, do so now and free yourself from the past. If you cannot, you are still living in the past, which will not create the best future for yourself.

What did you learn that will help you next time?

Do not let your fear of your past affect the outcome of your future. Live for what today has to offer, not what yesterday has taken away. There will always be obstacles in life, but we are confined mostly by the walls we create and build ourselves. What we see depends on how we view things. So instead, forget what you have lost and focus on what you have learned that will add to your life.

Life is full of uncontrollable circumstances, but the only thing we can control is how we choose to respond. When you really take the time to think about it, everything happening around us is of no matter and is meaningless up until we give it meaning. And the questions we ask ourselves generate the meaning we create.

In any situation, it is about choosing: Will I allow this to upset me or not? Will I choose to stay or walk away? Will I choose to make this bad or good? Will I choose to react or take the time to respond? Will I choose to yell or whisper? The final choice is always yours to make.

The bottom line here is the questions we ask ourselves shape our behaviors, and our behaviors can make a significant difference. In reality, we create our future every single day, and most of the illnesses we suffer come directly from our own uncontrollable behavior.

Which of these questions or views resonated the most with who you are? What do you do to stay mindful, grounded, and focused when problems appear in your life?

Affirmation

- Life is always about change, and I'm open to new thoughts to improve myself—always.

PATHWAY 30

Small Steps Toward Moving Ahead

The only way to make sense out of change is to plunge into it, move with it, and join the dance.

—Alan Watts

Positive Mini Habits Can Change Your Life and World

Diana: It was just after Christmas 2014, and like many others, I was thinking about how the year went. I realized I had more than enough room for improvement in too many areas of my life. Knowing that success rates for New Year's resolutions are usually low, I wanted to explore other options.

The last week of December, I decided that I wanted to get myself in better shape. My goal was to develop a forty-five-minute workout, although it seemed impossible to me at the time.

My motivation was low because I was always tired, and my guilt was making me feel worthless and stuck. I remembered a technique I read about that would change the way I looked at working out and change my life for the better.

The technique is to think the opposite of an idea you are stuck on. So, I looked at my forty-five-minute workout goal and the overwhelming exercise plan to get into better shape, and I thought about the opposite. You could say the opposite to me is the size of clothing I wanted to wear.

Therefore, I thought, *What if, instead of belittling myself, I just do one push-up?*

Initially, I pushed aside at the idea. *How silly to do a single push-up and act as if it means anything.* But when I continued to struggle with my bigger plans, I finally gave in to the idea and did one push-up, and because I was already in push-up position, I did a few more. After that, I felt warmed up, and I decided to try one jumping jack. And guess what. I ended up doing several more. Eventually, I had exercised for forty-five-minutes. I was amazed and thought to myself, *Did I just do a full workout due to a single push-up? Yes, I did!*

One push-up is all you need to start a positive workout habit.

I challenged many of my clients who wanted to be in better shape to do at least one push-up per day for a full year. Many people have had great success with it, and so have I. For the past three months, I have gone to a workout yoga class three times a week, and I am starting to feel better because it works.

I have always held a keen interest in psychology, and I read about it often due to the nature of my work. When I read about the studies on willpower, I learned that there is limited support—and that is when everything started making sense to me.

I could not do my forty-five-minute workout because my willpower was not strong enough or was always exhausted. But I could do one push-up and change it gradually into a forty-five-minute workout because it only required a tiny amount of willpower to start, but that was after my body and mind stopped resisting the idea. Without a doubt, this thought does not only apply to fitness but to any area of your life you wish to change. I believe I have found the perfect way to support this positive technique habit.

The importance of your habits.

To some degree, habits shape your behavior. Not only that, but they are also behaviors that you repeat daily, which become a part of your life. Habits are your foundation, and if your foundation is weak, you will not be happy with the way you live—much less be happy at all.

The reason we fail to change our lives and fail to add new habits is because we try to do too much at once. Make it simple. If your new habit requires more willpower than you can give, you will fail. If your new habit requires less willpower than you can achieve, you will succeed.

This can also be applied when you are tired and your willpower is burnt out. Therefore, you can continue with what needs to be done.

One thing I have been wanting to do more of is continue writing my book. It is so therapeutic for me and I love writing, so it is a must to put it into practice. When I found that I was not writing as much as I wanted to, I figured out how to combine the power of the one push-up challenge with a habit plan.

Changing your life with positive mini habits.

Mini habits are exactly as they sound. First, you choose a desired habit or a change you would like to make. It could be thinking more positively, writing five hundred words a day, or reading one book per week. I've have had success doing three positive mini habits at once.

After that, you shrink these habits down until they are small enough to handle. When you say the requirement out loud, it is so small it sounds silly.

Here are some of my positive mini habits:

- Write five hundred words per day in my book.
- Write five hundred words per day to better my thoughts.
- Read two pages of a book per day.

Now this is easy, right? I could complete this list in ten minutes total or less. So far, I have met these daily requirements 100 percent of the time and then some. I have actually written one to one thousand words and read ten to thirty pages per day for the past twelve days. Prior to this, I was not reading at all and writing very little.

It works because your brain falls for the bait. It starts to think, *Oh, only five hundred words? I can write that. That's easy!* Then, you notice good things happen.

Ideas for daily mini habits:

- Compliment *one* person.

- Think *two* positive thoughts.

- Meditate for *five* minutes.

- Name *three* things you are grateful for.

- Do *one* push-up.

- Write *five hundred* words.

- Read *two* pages.

- Do *six* jumping jacks.

- Go outside and take *fifty* steps.

- Drink *one* glass of water.

You can change nearly any area of your life one positive mini habit at a time. It is easier than you think.

When you remove the pressure and expectations from your thoughts, you allow yourself to start. What positive mini habit or habits will you start today to better your life?

Affirmation

- I end procrastination by taking small steps. This allows to complete the tasks I want to complete.

PATHWAY 31

Dare to Compare

Everything in life is easier when you don't concern
yourself with what everybody else is doing.

—Shaun Nestor

Using Comparisons for Growth

At one point or another, we all struggle with comparison, although it
is something that self-help wisdom advises us to avoid. It also allows
us to know where we fit in the world.

Diana: Most of the time, when we compare ourselves to others, we
do so from an ego-based perspective and find ourselves or others
lacking. This approach does not benefit anyone involved, and this was
my main experience of comparison. I also had the belief that healthy
people do not compare themselves to other people, so I would judge
myself seriously when I noticed I was doing so.

So, I struggled. First, I needed to stop comparing myself to other
people. Then, I shifted my focus to self-acceptance and self-kindness

to accept the fact that this is something I do and judging myself for this does not help me in any way.

Are you focusing on the facts or the feeling and things you attach to the facts?

Through my experiences, I have realized that it is not so much the comparison itself that is unhealthy but how I approach it. In other words, the act of comparison is not the problem; it is the meaning we attach to what we find.

When I notice that I am comparing myself to other people, I have a choice to make: Do I use this comparison as a tool for positive change or a tool for self-destruction? I, of course, choose to have a positive change.

Use Comparison as a Tool for a Better Life

This question came up recently when I was talking with a couple of friends I have known all my life about how things were going in the Silva corporate businesses. One of them shared that she had just had her best month yet and earned more than ever before. In that moment, I was both happy for her and deeply envious of her.

I had been working really hard, and although I felt good about how things were going, I compared how much I was earning to how much she was earning and found myself falling seriously short. On an intellectual level, I reasoned with myself that money was not everything, but on an emotional level, I compared myself to her badly. I started questioning myself about what I was doing wrong, feeling self-doubt, and digging myself deeper, which left me with a general sense that I was not doing enough.

I recognized this was not serving me at all; therefore, I spoke to one of my sisters about the experience. When I explained that I could not even imagine making that much and that I was wondering how she had done that herself, she asked, "Did you ask her?"

As soon as she said that to me, it seemed like such an obvious thing to do. But I did not because I had felt ashamed. In that moment of time, my ego-based comparison had robbed me of the opportunity to learn something new and positive, to be inspired, and to grow. And that, I have realized, is the choice we face daily. When we compare ourselves to others, it is usually because they have something we want, they are doing something we wish to do, or there is something we want to have, do, or be.

When we notice that and notice the uncomfortable feeling of envy arising, we then have a decision to make. We can beat ourselves up over the space between where we are now and where they are now, or we can ask ourselves the obvious: What is this comparison telling me about what I am wanting and/or needing right now? And what can I learn from this person or situation to get myself closer to where I want to be?

One of these opportunities is based on ego gratification and external validation; the other is based on self-compassion and a desire to live the best life we can. Making this choice is not so easy to do at the moment, but it is possible.

Viewing comparison as an opportunity is an act of self-kindness. It lifts the burden of not being enough and provides a chance for growth and reconnection, more so if the person you are comparing yourself to is someone you can reach out to and ask. For example, you may inquire, "I would love to be able to do what you are doing. Do you have any advice to share on how to be successful like you?" Never be ashamed to ask because you just never know who wants to share their success secrets.

Maybe one day I will realize that I no longer need to compare myself to others. In the meantime, I accept that this is something I do for strength and positivity.

How do you deal with comparison in your life?

Affirmation

- I compare myself with others in order to find ways to better myself.

PATHWAY 32

If You Cannot Control It, Do Not Complain

Being happy doesn't mean that everything is perfect. It means
that you've decided to look beyond the imperfections.

—Gerard Way

How to Be Happier with What Life Brings

We all complain, and many of us do it nonstop. Even if you argue that
you are the happiest person in the world, you still complain sometimes.
And sometimes we complain without even realizing it, but rarely is it
ever helpful. Sure, a common complaint can bond two people who
may have nothing in common, but too much complaining would just
break down the relationship.

Diana: For example, I once had a friend who constantly griped about
her health, her family, her relationships, her college, and more. Every
time I hung out with her, I felt drained afterward. No matter what
I said or did, it never seemed to cheer her up. There is no arguing
that she was going through a tough time, but her negative attitude

certainly made matters worse. Eventually, we grew apart because it was more than I wanted to handle at the time.

So, what happens if you are the one stuck in the negative attitude? We have all been there at one time or another. I know I sure have. There are days when everything seems to go wrong, and complaining is the easiest thing for me to do. It is easier to complain than to fix the problem, like quitting a job or having a serious talk with your better half or someone who you clash with. But I found that you can make the change happen when you put your mind toward a more positive outlook and force yourself to end complaining, which is possible to do because everything in life is always possible to change for the better.

Here are some ideas for how to stop complaining by doing away with the negative thoughts you have in mind and focus on finding solutions.

Change the way you think.

Of course, this is definitely easier said than done because our brains intend to lean toward the negative side of life. Just like the saying goes, we are bothered by the thorns that come in a rose bush instead of being amazed by the sight of the beautiful roses and their fragrance.

This definitely requires a new way of being mindful. When you find yourself thinking or saying a negative comment about something or someone, stop and force yourself to say something positive instead. And if you need help, ask a dependable friend or family member to stop you when you complain and allow that person to help you to see the positive side in the situation. It will bring you amazing feelings when doing so.

Release your feelings with positive intentions.

When you constantly ignore your negative thoughts, they could add up at the end of the day. If you are really going through a rough time, do not be afraid to share your feelings with a close friend or family member or seek professional help if need be. You should never feel ashamed of reaching out to someone for help when you have confusing negative feelings coming to mind. Remember that it matters not how you seek help so long as you do because there is nothing wrong when seeking for help.

Practice yoga as much as you can.

Yoga is a great way to exercise, relax, and be mindful. Yoga focuses on breathing, movement, and meditation and helps you to control your mind and body. Our minds often race a million miles in many directions to no avail. Yoga can help you calm your negative chattering thoughts, which allows your mind and body to be stronger and positive with your intentions.

Learn to be less judgmental.

We often complain about others because we think they are not up to our standards. Once you stop judging people without knowing what is happening in their lives, you will most likely complain less about the things people do.

For example, constantly complaining about the service in a restaurant is not helpful. You do not know what kind of a day your waiter or waitress has had or what problems that person may be going through in life. If you put yourself in the other person's shoes for a minute, you may be a little kinder and relaxed about the situation. Learn to be open-minded and mindful before judging anyone or anything.

Create a grateful list.

At the end of the day, take the time to think of all the great things and amazing people in your life and list them in your journal. Doing so will allow you to put any silly complaints behind you. Staying grateful is not an easy thing to do, especially when negative thoughts get in the way. Yet everything is possible to change for the better. So stay faithful and grateful with yourself every day.

Accept responsibility.

If something is bothering you, you have to either fix it or accept that nothing can be done at the moment, so what is the sense of complaining? Complaining is a passive activity. Change your complaining into positive action in order to solve the problem or simply accept the problem and give your mind rest. Better yet, give it something positive to focus on.

Find what passion makes you happy.

Sometimes listing your passions can be easy to do. For example, you can easily list out all the hobbies you enjoy. Though, at times, it requires you to think deeper in order to have a better understanding of what you have already gone through. Are you constantly complaining about your job? If you are, maybe it is time to make a hard yet positive decision to move on to another job or career. Discover what your biggest complaints are about, and see whether you can change the situation to make yourself happy.

Make sure to always take care of yourself.

Stress along with a busy lifestyle can often take over our lives, which then can break down our positive spirits. Learn to take time out from your life just for you. Make time to see the family movie you ordered for this weekend, take a hot steam shower, go to a hot yoga class, get a massage, or do whatever relaxes and energizes you. It could just put you in a new frame of mind, and who knows what would be next.

Ask yourself this simple question: When speaking to yourself or to others, what would you speak about? Would you complain or be happy? If it were me, I would choose to be happy while focusing on the positive side of life and being kind to everything around me. Remember, that is a choice we each have because no one else makes it.

What is your best positive way to stop complaining?

Affirmation

- I catch myself when I feel the need to complain about anything outside of my control.

PATHWAY 33

Being Creative

Creativity is Intelligence Having Fun.

—Albert Einstein

Developing Creativity

Diana: I believe that creativity and spirituality are somehow connected to each other. By spirituality, I do not mean religion; I am referring to the human spirit, our own source, the place that is deep within our hearts that feels connected to life itself. This beautiful place cannot be described by words because it is something that can only be felt by the heart itself.

Being creative is simply relaxing into that place and connecting with your higher intelligence, which is the source that is within you. It is a gift that is within each of us, waiting to be discovered. We all come to this world as talented beings because we all have access to the same infinite source. We are all richly supplied, naturally. When we act from a place of creation, we are in a place of abundance where there are no bounds in life. Limitations and lack only come when we act from a place of competition and comparison.

To me, there is no such thing as being more creative because you are already a creative being. However, you can practice becoming more in tune or aware of that creative, positive energy surrounding you that you have unlimited access to.

Here are some ideas I practice daily that helped me cultivate creativity:

Be relaxed.

Take a moment to do something that makes you happy, that brings your heart joy, or that you love to do daily while you surround yourself with the energy that comes with it, which centers and grounds you completely from head to toe. It could simply be meditating daily, taking a long walk at a park, going for a sweet swim, reading something that puts you in a positive and happy mood, or journaling your day and thoughts. Do what makes you happy because you only have one life to live, so you might as well live it to its fullest while you can.

Practice gratitude.

Thinking about all things you are grateful for produces a positive energy flow and vibration. As you feel the love in your heart for all the wonderful blessings and gifts in your life, you will instantly relax and feel all the love that comes from deep within. In that moment of warmth and love, you are open to creative energy where ideas are born.

Work with your imagination.

Imagination is highly visual. Therefore, it is helpful to practice seeing vivid images with your eyes closed. I always do my best to see everything in my mind first. Try it out yourself. Close your eyes and imagine that you are in a scene, any scene you desire for that matter. Okay, now that you have picked out your ideal scene, practice seeing the details of your situation in this scene. See the colors, feel the textures, and touch something for memory. Use all of your sensing facilities to full capacity. So what does it feel like? What do you hear? What do you smell? What is the temperature like? Have fun using your imagination while you are there.

Live for the moment.

For example, every outstanding musician or singer will tell you that when he or she is creating great music, there are no thoughts in mind but to be completely in the moment and experiencing the flow of creation. Practice what present moment awareness is about by giving your full attention to whatever you are doing, be it eating, washing dishes, or making your bed. Meditating daily helps tremendously when doing so.

Always do your best to stay inspired.

Practice seeing beautiful things that bring you joy emotionally. Look through a book that contains thought-provoking images, go to an art gallery, read something inspirational, or talk to someone who knows how to bring you tranquility. Just do something that will make a change in your life for the better.

Choose to see alternatives.

Always be curious. Practice asking yourself how to do something differently. When seeing a solution to a problem, ask yourself, what are some other alternative ways to doing this better? Develop the mental attitude that there are many other ways to achieve what is needed even when it seems impossible. Just keep in mind that in life everything is possible to change for the better. It is just a matter of attitude and time.

Be open-minded to what comes to mind.

Never push aside any idea that comes your way and never make judgments about it either. Appreciate any idea that comes to you, even the ones that seem silly or simple. By doing so, you encourage more creative ideas to surface, which always comes from within each of us. So stay open-minded to the possibilities of what life can bring.

Write it down on paper.

Start writing ideas down in your journal or any paper for that matter. But write down everything that comes to mind. For example, random words, phrases, ideas, and thoughts are good, and yet there may be times when all you can do is doodle or draw lines to connect ideas and so on. But when a clear inspiration comes to mind, follow it to see what the next step would be. If you suddenly have a different idea, write it down somewhere on the page or even on a new page. This is how I construct my quote-of-the-day emails. I start with ideas and points. Though at times it can really be crappy points at the beginning, once I am in the flow of it, the quote of the day will take shape right before my eyes. There is nothing hard about creating. All you have to do is take the first step by allowing your creative mind to have fun while following the source that is within us each.

Allow me to ask you … When do you feel most creative?

Affirmation

- I use my mind to create the world that I envision.

PATHWAY 34

Taking Action via Motivation

Take action! An inch of movement will bring you
closer to your goals than a mile of intention.
—Dr. Steve Maraboli

Motivating Yourself to Take Action

Powerful motivation comes in understanding that you can achieve
anything you truly desire in your heart. It is the knowledge that
you are destined to fulfill your every goal, which encourages you to
change.

The decision is the first step toward change. Regardless of the
decision, every change requires some kind of action. Do you find
it challenging at times to motivate yourself in taking action? There
are many times I catch my mind making excuses, and occasionally I
succeed in avoiding the action I need to take altogether.

Helpful Pointers That Will Keep You Motivated

Why and what.

Start with the end in mind. To achieve a goal, it is important to clearly define what goal you have in mind. How do you know when you have achieved the goal? Mark a day and date for when this goal should be met. Once you have your goal in mind, it is important to understand the *why*. Why you are aiming for that goal? Ask yourself what are the motivating factors behind wanting that goal? Is it for your family or your kids? Why? For what reason must you achieve this goal? Why? Do your best to answer the, who, what, why, where, when, and how to better understand why you want that goal.

Break it down into small, achievable tasks.

It is very easy, and human, to be overwhelmed by the pure effort and energy involved in achieving a big goal. This is magnified if the goal consists of many unknowns or if the process of achieving it is a long one. We tell ourselves it is impossible or it is too much work, and then we give up even before we take any action toward the goal.

Diana: I have found it very helpful to split the main goal into several mini goals. Then I break each mini goal into a series of steps. For each step, break it down further into smaller, measurable, and achievable tasks that can take a few hours or less. This will make the goal appear manageable. Achieving one task after another builds confidence and momentum, and before you know it, the end result will be in sight. Personally, I feel rewarded and more motivated just by crossing tasks off with a black marker as I complete them. Therefore, make sure to put it on paper.

Take a small step at a time.

Even the smallest first step forward will help create momentum toward change. It is like it is said when I read a borrowed book from my friend Bob Proctor, "Start doing the thing to have energy to do the thing." When I read this quote, it is like a light bulb turn on. So from now on, whenever I do not want to do something that I know will help me, I trick myself into thinking I am just going to start it, and it will only take a few minutes of my time. And once I start something, I normally finish and achieve the task.

Always reward and celebrate what you have achieved.

Give yourself small rewards for every small achievement you complete. Then celebrate when you reach each mini goal. I always reward myself when achieving my mini goals, for that tells me I am moving in the right direction. So I either buy myself chia iced tea or a new book to read. Do whatever makes you happy. For that reason, look back at what you have done, enjoy it, embrace it, and give yourself a pat on the back for a job well done. I like to exaggerate this step by doing a happy dance. I do silly moves that tend to make others and myself laugh. By doing so, my body moves, I am smiling, and my mind will create positive connections with achieving my mini goals to being happy.

The Pros and Cons of Pain and Pleasure

Have you ever noticed that you are more inclined to avoid pain than to gain pleasure? For example, we all know the benefits of eating healthy and exercising, but this benefit alone often is not enough to motivate us to taking action. But, if your doctor tells you that you must live a healthier lifestyle, or you might take ill in the very near future, you are more likely to make the change. Here is a visualization technique I learned at a very young age; it is called the mirror of the mind and is found in our Silva Life System program.

Close your eyes take several deep breaths. Then count yourself down from ten to one. Place a blue-framed mirror in front of you. In the mirror, visualize yourself in two years without taking the actions to reach your goal. See yourself the way the situation is: unhappy, unhealthy, and with pain. Do this for less than a minute and then intensify the feeling. Feel the heaviness on your back. Do this for a couple of seconds more and then relax as you erase the image.

Then move the mirror ever so slightly to the left, change the frame to white, and visualize yourself having achieved your goal. What do you look like? How do you feel? How are you celebrating? See and feel the benefits it has provided. Now, let that feeling intensify. Do this for fifteen minutes, but before coming out, claim and energize your end result.

Then later in the day, when entering for the second time, you only see the end result in the white-framed mirror. There is where you can always energize it some more, or you can place that image in the blue-framed mirror to improve it some more by taking it to the next mini goal. Do this until you have reached your mini goals, which, in due time, will direct you to achieving your main goal.

Inspiration Does Help

Being around motivated people does help to inspire us into taking action. Be with people who are always aligned with their actions toward their goals. Being around these people can be contagious, and their energy will impact you. If you do not have such people in your life, go to a motivational speakers' conference. Listen to the outstanding speakers' voices. It can create enough energy to pump you up. I highly recommend you listen to any motivational speaker, such as my sister Laura Silva Quesada, Les Brown, Bob Proctor, or the late Louise Hay.

Tell me, what do you do to motivate yourself?

Affirmation

- I take action in order to keep myself motivated in every aspect of my life.

PATHWAY 35

Making Decisions

Pursue one great decisive aim with force and determination.
—Carl von Clausewitz

Steps to Be Decisive

Life, at times, can feel overwhelming, more so when we face many options, pending decisions, and countless unknowns. Making a decision can seem difficult and even scary; when you consider the long list of consequences your decision will have, your mind becomes clouded. Creating confusion, therefore, is helpless by the fear of the consequences. Your mind can easily become caught in the confusion of reaching a conclusion, yet I know you will find that a decision is as easy or as complicated as you choose it to be.

The path we choose in life is shaped by the decisions we make every moment. If we are not conscious in the decisions we make, then we feel as if we are endlessly drifting in our unconscious, feeling helplessly hopeful, yet afraid to face the unknown. Do your best to break through that barrier, take control, and decide to be decisive instead. The understanding to make a clear decision comes with the choice and belief that you are decisive, meaning determined and certain. Clarity has power, and making an unquestionable decision gives you energy. This absolute energy will attract the resources and support you need to carry out that decision. When you are clear and sharp about your decision, others will not second-guess you; instead, they will back you up. There is no magic in developing the ability to be decisive. It is simply a mindset—a mental attitude that comes with practice and persistence.

The following are techniques used to gain clarity and to become more decisive:

Believe in yourself and in all that you do.

Tell yourself that you are decisive and determined to achieve your goals. Stop telling yourself and other people that you are indecisive. It is a great story, but it does not help you much if you really want to make fast, firm decisions.

Visualize everything beforehand.

Visualize yourself as a confident and decisive person who is able to make quick and firm decisions. For example, close your eyes and see yourself in decisive action—actions that are important to make. What do you look like on the outside? How do you feel on the inside? All of these feelings play a major role in life.

No bad decisions are ever made.

Realize that there are no bad decisions in life. Everything is a learning lesson to go through. Have faith that no matter which decision you make, there is a beautiful lesson behind it and you will gain knowledge from it, regardless of its outcome. Besides, action will always beat not taking action at all.

Be brave and just go for it.

Never be afraid to make mistakes. You will become better at deciding situations, information, and your emotions as you go. Plus, the more you do it, the better you become. Therefore, let all your fears go.

Have faith by following your instincts.

Learn to listen to your instincts. Trust what your belly is feeling. Your heart knows it all. Start by paying close attention to what your inner voice is telling you. Realize that your whole being is always telling you what is best for you and your well-being.

Step back to see the possibilities in life.

Extend the possibilities by considering your hidden action plans and creatively brainstorm other solutions. You have the control to set the pace for the success you wish to achieve.

Set a date and time.

Force yourself to make decisions due to a tight deadline. You do not actually need a lot of time to make reasonable decisions. You just think you do. Trust in yourself. Setting a time limit will allow you to achieve or get closer to your goal.

Persistence is a must to practice.

Force yourself to make fast decisions often. In due time, you will become better. Start with small decisions such as what to have for dinner, what to do on the weekend, what to plan for next week, and so on. Being persistent leads to achieving your goals.

Thinking out loud allows clarity.

On a piece of paper simply define the title to this quote and write down your decisions and action plan, followed by any other thoughts or concerns you have in mind. Just keep writing down all of your thoughts on paper as they come to mind. Do not edit what you have written; just write it all down one by one. And never worry yourself if your thoughts are unclear or do not flow. Just keep going with the flow as you allow yourself to release.

So decide today to be decisive or not.

Affirmation

- I trust my inner wisdom to guide me toward every decision with ease.

PATHWAY 36

Keeping the Focus—
One Step at a Time

Your life is controlled by what you focus on.
—Tony Robbins

Focus Your Attention Completely

Diana: I recently sat down to chat with some of my siblings who are highly enthusiastic achievers. All of them have multiple goals in mind. This encouraging gathering revolved around the theme of how do I turn my goal into a reality? I deeply love and admire them and their energy dearly, but it became clear to me why they were not seeing all their desired results. To me, it is like they were trying to do too much all at once, which might not always be possible on many levels of life.

Regardless of what others may think, we can have it all if we want it all. Therefore, learn to work with the limited amount of energy and time you have. Even if we think we can achieve it all while we are at our highest state of mind, when reality comes to mind, we find that attempting to achieve it all at once will end up in exhaustion and many times disconnection from our inner selves. Instead of attempting to achieve it all, why not strive to achieve what is most important to us? How about striving to be fulfilled and happy? How about striving for personal well-being and positive growth?

Stop Doing Too Much in One Day

Because it is a known fact that we have a limited amount of resources such as attention, energy, and time, how we divide our resources greatly affects the success of our desired outcome. The more focused we are at any one goal, the more energy is concentrated into that desired thing.

For example, put your attention to the sharpness of an arrow. An arrow can be sharp because energy has been focused on the point. Therefore, the more focused the energy is at the point, the sharper the arrow will be, the faster it will go, and the easier it will hit the target. If energy is not focused at the point, its sharpness could end up somewhere else and/or fail to hit the target at all. A dull arrow may be good for having fun, but if your goal was to hit the target with a powerful punch, you have missed the desired outcome.

When we try to do too much, it is as if we are trying to sharpen too many arrows all at once within a limited time. We toss around between the sharpening of the different arrows, resulting in not one arrow being sharpened enough to be considered useful. We can be more effective if we spend our time and focus our energy sharpening one arrow at a time and moving on to next arrow only when the first one has reached its desired outcome. When I refer to an arrow, I mean your goals and the attention you need to give to your desired goals, which is your passion.

One example of doing too much is having one too many goals that you are trying to achieve in the same short period of time. The words *too many* are subjective, and we each have our individual understanding of what that means. Though there are exceptions to this also, and there are people who are outstanding at multitasking, I for sure know that I am not one of those people.

If you are like me, then maybe you can relate to the feeling of doing too much all at once and how that tension can take us away from what matters to you most.

Steps on how to adjust your life situations as you prioritize and balance your lifestyle:

Nonstop mental chattering.

Thinking constantly about the things you still have to do will clutter your inner space. They become mental noises and are very distracting in life. They are chattering nonstop and ready to take over if you allow it to. Therefore, we must learn to control the constant chattering thoughts in order to achieve our goals in a timely manner.

Not able to focus.

When we are distracted by too many things or goals, we feel overwhelmed, our focus is distributed, and things appear cloudy from our perspective. In this state of mind, it is harder to focus on what you are doing, much less think clearly or make fast and rational decisions when fear and worries want to take over. So when this happens, just remember who is in control. You are!

Not having a personal life is like not having success at all.

We can become consumed by all the external achievements we are reaching to obtain our main goal for the price to a title called success. But by doing so, we forget to experience the joy that should come from the success. We forget to look after ourselves, our health, and our personal lives. We become unbalanced and unclear about what should be and what should not be. Yet, in many cases, it is part of life until we learn the way to a balanced life.

Do not allow exhaustion to make its way to you.

When our energies are not properly managed, we feel exhausted and our bodies can take ill. This can physically manifest in different ways. For me, exhaustion leads to lower back pain, sleepless nights, and dehydration. These things, at times, can get the best of us, but you are stronger than you think. Give it your all as long as you take care of your needs too.

Feeling guilty.

When we become too consumed, we tend to underestimate how long things will take, and this can cause feelings of being overwhelmed. We commit ourselves to this overwhelming situation and unconsciously set ourselves up for failure. When we realize that we have not done what we are set to do, we become subject to the guilt inflicted by our own minds. Therefore, we tend to sabotage ourselves. This can be so destructive to our motivation and self-esteem. So, watch what you think, keeping in mind to never belittle yourself for what you are going through in life. Life should always be seen with an open mind no matter what it brings.

Relationships and the pain.

When our attention is fully occupied with too many goals, we do not have room for other important life areas, such as improving and maintaining relationships with people we love. Too many hurts can stop anyone from developing that connection with people in general, but we must keep in mind that we learn from each other, so relationships with others are crucial.

Unsatisfied.

When we have too much on our list of things to do, we are constantly chasing after the things we have not achieved yet and forget to celebrate what we have achieved. That usually happens because our attention is spread out so thin that we cannot really excel at achieving any of our goals. So, we become dissatisfied. This is similar to self-inflicted guilt. Remember that this feeling is not at all helpful to a healthy self-esteem.

My best friend's story.

The other day I received an email from my best friend. She said about two years ago she was so enthusiastic and ready to take on the world to achieve something exciting. She went on to say that she saw other people's successes and attempted to do the same. The problem was that she was finding inspiration from several people more experienced than she was. She saw their results and then attempted to do all of her goals at once just like they did because she was so ready.

Keep in mind that it is a must to feel inspired and take massive action because not having a clear, positive, and focused mind can cause anyone to lose sight, and that was exactly what happened to her. She also felt exhausted, was unhappy, and lived an unbalanced lifestyle, and she disliked how it made her feel.

But then suddenly things started to turn around when she remembered what I had told her many years ago about life being about joy, compassion, and love. Life is about experiencing, sharing, and spreading compassion and love to everything and everyone no matter what.

So I told her, "Pick yourself up off the floor, focus on a step-by-step plan, and then give your complete focus to one goal at a time." When she did that, she started living and achieving her goals. That is when her life became beautiful, and that is when she started to live life to its fullest.

Be choosy when you start focusing on your goals.

Does that mean I am to drop everything and only focus on working on one goal at a time?

What I am advising you is that, in my personal experience, I've found that having one main goal to focus on and completely give your all to will give you a higher chance of success. By doing so, you are able to work on multiple goals at the same time; some people can pull it off without any stress in the way, while others find it challenging.

Learn to become sensitive to your inner state of mind and observe the results carefully. If you are not getting the results you are looking for or you are experiencing stress, you may be doing too much at once. Consider cutting back a little and focus on one goal or thing at a time. If you can achieve one goal, then aim for two goals, but if at any given time you are overwhelming yourself, cut back to one goal at a time. The point here is to achieve your goals one by one without stress.

If I were to focus completely on only one goal, how can I improve in other areas of my life?

I always look forward to the ideas that come to mind more than the important areas of my life. And many times, creating one main goal for each one of them is a good thing. Yet most of the time when there is more than one goal in each area, it will usually result in failure. My personal areas, which always need improvement, are relationships at all levels, spirituality, personal business and growth, and physical health. Creating time for each major area is a must, and as you do so, keep in mind that life is a never-ending process of improvements. I am always looking forward to working in combining all of those areas into my daily life, which so far has been a little challenging for me, though I have no doubts that one day soon it will happen. For example, at the beginning of each week, I would work on two areas I wanted to focus on for the week. I would focus on my main goal, such as relationships and spirituality, personal and business growth, or physical health. But keep in mind not to work on all of them at the same time.

There is so much I want to achieve. How do I choose what priority to focus on?

Choosing what to focus on can be a challenging task on its own, especially if you have already invested time, money, and energy in other projects. Prioritizing is a good thing to do.

Below are a few things to help you get started:

List life areas that need improvements.

In your journal, write out a list of important areas of your life you wish to change for the better. Then write down some ideas on how to improve those things step by step, leading you to achieve your main goal. You can apply any of the pointers that were explained above.

Determine the outcome of your goals.

For each life area you described above, list out goals you would like to achieve or improve in for each of them. Do this in your journal or on a regular piece of paper. Make sure that each goal is described with a measurable time frame. For example, instead of saying, "I want to exercise," say, "I do yoga three times a week." But remember to list out your goals in the present tense, as if you have already achieved them all.

Add meaning as to why this goal is important to you.

For each of your goals, it is a must to understand why each one of them is important to you. What will you gain if you achieve this goal?

Write one word that will describe it next to each goal you set. You can write down money as a description, but it is too vague and general. What will that money mean to you? What will it translate to in your life? Maybe you will achieve comfort or security or happiness. What does achieving this goal mean to you at the most basic level of life? This exercise will help you understand the energy behind doing what you do.

Prioritizing is a must in life.

Now it is time to go through your goals in each area and select which is most important to you. Which do you want to work on first and most? And which gets you excited? When prioritizing, it helps to follow your passion. Look at each item and ask the question, "If I had all the money in the world, would I be improving on this goal?" If you answered yes, make sure you mark it as a priority on your list.

Now review all of the items marked with priority, and ask yourself, "If I could be granted the realization of just one goal and I need to choose it now, which would I choose?" What was the first thing that came to mind? Listen to what comes to mind, which is your heart and your gut reaction. Place the number 1 next to this goal. This is your highest and first priority in this life area. You must learn to listen to what your gut—your heart—is telling you. When doing so, life will always be beautiful.

When and how do you plan to achieve each goal?

For each goal you plan to focus on, make sure the end result is clearly defined with a step-by-step plan and that is it achieved within a measurable time frame. Add a date of when you will achieve it. Make the goal achievable but slightly more challenging than comfortable. Write the goal down in present tense on a piece of paper or in your journal. Stick that piece of paper on a wall where you will see it daily and throughout the day. Remember to review it often. List out a step-by-step plan and go straight into massive action forward—today.

Begin your goal with the end result in mind.

What will you do once you achieve it? What goal is next on your list? Will you start on another goal, or will you improve on the one you are currently achieving? Understanding your deadlines and strategies, along with planning out your next step, can add clarity to understanding your goals.

Do away with goals that have less priority.

For all the other goals that are not marked as your first priority, do your best to do away with them, as they might not bring you great success in return. Or do away with tasks for goals that are not working or that are not worth moving forward. Just because you committed yourself to doing something does not mean that it must be done right now. If something is not in alignment with your life goals, drop it or put it to the side. Always clearly communicate to yourself and with others because being honest will save a lot of wasted energy in the long run.

Creating enough time is crucial.

If you were told your goal would be granted if you gave it enough attention and action, how much time would you be willing to commit to achieving your goal? For example, every other day of the week set two hours aside to dedicate to working on this particular goal. Do this until you reach your main goal. But keep in mind to set aside some time to review your progress, goals, and deadlines for the following week. If you follow those same steps, I can say you too can achieve all your goals.

What is your main goal right now? What life areas are important to you that need changing for the better?

Affirmation

- When planning my goals, I stay grounded and focused when I take on challenges a little at a time.

PATHWAY 37

Turning Fear into Action

Pain must enter into its glorified life of memory
before it can turn into compassion.

—George Eliot

Fear and the Pain That Comes with It

Diana: My son's pet fish died. He had a big, beautiful orange-and-white goldfish. Four weeks prior, it was swimming around in the pond we have outside, happy as can be. But then suddenly the fish was less active. Then it stopped eating. Then he was gone. As we buried it in the yard, my son's first thought was that he never wanted to have another pet fish ever again. Suddenly, awareness kicked in, and I realized that my son's thought was triggered by fear of experiencing loss or an unpleasant circumstance.

This is how our minds work after we go through a hurtful situation. We subconsciously avoid anything we think caused our pain. This instinct of self-security can protect us from repeating mistakes and experiencing pain, but it can also prevent us from living life to the fullest.

One of my friends accepted a job that required her to relocate constantly. After the fourth move, she decided it was not worth making new friends in her new town because it seemed to be a less hurtful option to distance herself from others. Focusing entirely on work and the ones she holds dearly, which includes staying in touch with her best friends, such as me, does not complete what she is missing in her life.

My nephew swore to never have another dog after losing his fourteen-year-old pet to an illness. And by doing so, he does not have to deal with the loss of another family member, as he was still mourning his loss years later.

I have seen one too many who, after a traumatic experience with marriage, felt that the mere thought of starting a new romantic relationship would make them physically ill because they did not want to be hurt again; therefore, they would distrust everyone they met, which prevented them from welcoming new people into their lives. And that normally happens until they realize that their sense of self-protection had become their biggest obstacle to creating new and meaningful connections.

Let go of the fear of being hurt again and open your heart and mind to what life brings your way. Remember these things:

A *full life is made of lots of experiences, both pleasant and unpleasant.*

Job position and/or opportunities change daily; people, which includes our pets can become ill and/or die. Relationships at times do end.

We need to accept that we are not always in control, and sometimes things will not go our way. By doing so, it will allow you to let go of the anxiety and stress that arise from resisting life circumstances. When you stop resisting, your mind will be clear enough to find solutions to your problems.

Fear based on painful experiences will not protect you in life.

Why is that? Because living in fear is already living in pain. Instead of avoiding what needs to be learned or completed, look for ways to stay joyful.

When I focused on personality and what people can offer, I started looking for people who have behaviors that reflect these qualities. When doing so, I started to meet amazing people who became my eternal and trusted friends.

Take responsibility to control your life again.

Ask yourself, "How do my thoughts and behaviors contribute to what is happening to me now?" Remember, the past will not repeat itself if you learn from the difficulty it brought you in the first place, so take control of your thoughts about the situation. Even if you feel that you did not take part in the challenge you experienced, you can still take responsibility for your attitude and feelings about what happened. You can choose to move on, or you can dwell on what is happening.

For example, my friend could choose to apply for a job that does not make her move so often, or she could view being relocated as an exciting opportunity to make new friends all over the country. My nephew could cherish the memory of his previous pet by giving a new dog all the love and care that all creatures deserve, which, in return, would give him gratifying feelings of love. When I let go of my limiting thoughts, I started to see life through a different lens and welcomed new people who were aligned with my values and appreciated me for who I am.

Self-preservation combined with conscious awareness brings positive results.

Become aware of your negative thoughts as soon as they come to mind and have the objective perspective of an observer. This will prevent you from being controlled by fear, which will then allow you to tap into your intuition.

Allow yourself to learn from the past and then let it go. Learn to leave the hurt and pain behind and learn to move forward so you can enjoy the unlimited, amazing abundance that life has to offer!

Hope you live a life of abundance and all that you have ever dreamed of.

Affirmation

- I utilize my fear and any negative thinking as motivation to change anything and everything for the better.

PATHWAY 38

Believe in Yourself

Everybody is a genius. But if you judge a fish by its ability to climb a tree, it will live its whole life believing that it is stupid.

—Albert Einstein

Better Self-Esteem

You know you are smart and capable, which means you can achieve great things in life. You have dreams of going places and doing things, not just simple things but incredible, fulfilling things. Yet you might not be reaching for those goals. You are striving to achieve your dreams, yet something could be stopping you. You know you're capable, but something may be preventing you from taking action.

Most of us deal with low self-esteem. It is the belief that we are not good enough. It is those deceptive thoughts that wrap around us, saying, "You are not worthy, capable, or as good as others are."

Here are some suggestions to help overcome low self-esteem:

Accept it for what it is.

This is a simple yet challenging approach. It is easy to say, "I accept it," and yet it is harder to do. The thing to remember here is that when you fight something, you are giving it power. When someone starts an argument and you argue back, you fuel that person's anger as well as your own. One of the quickest and easiest ways to release the tension is to validate the other person. You can say, "Yes, I hear what you're saying," even if you don't agree. That person's anger is released, and it has nowhere to go. You have then expressed acceptance.

The same holds true in accepting low self-esteem. When you feel it, close your eyes and look within. What do you feel? Where in your body do you feel this energy? What does it look like? Pretend you are a doctor examining your own body and feelings. Get curious and start observing. If you do this for a minute or two, you will feel a sense of calmness and acceptance, causing the power to be released. With practice, you will begin to think, *It is just my self-esteem*, and you will be able to deal with it.

Look forward to nurturing yourself.

Make a final decision to nurture your body with real food and exercise because you deserve it. Nurture your soul by doing the things you love and be around people who make you feel good. Nurture your emotions by going out with people you love and enjoy being around and entertain each other with what makes you laugh. Taking action to love yourself in this manner will boost your self-esteem as well as others'. But always keep in mind that everything starts with you first.

Control your thoughts at all times.

You can control your mind just as you control your body. You know those crazy thoughts that come to mind from time to time? The ones you do not listen to because they are wacky? Well, we all have them, and most of the time we listen to them. That happens because we set the bar too low. And at the same time, we need to do away with the thoughts that do us no good, especially if they are unhelpful. Those self-doubting thoughts can do so much harm. The next time you have one of those thoughts, stop yourself and think as you move on to a more positive thought. And if you find yourself thinking, *I can't do this,* thank yourself for thinking that thought. Then consciously think to yourself, *How in the world can I achieve it?*

Trigger points can make a world of a difference.

Consider whether certain things that you do or are involved in trigger your negative thoughts and feelings. If you always feel low self-esteem doing certain activities or in certain situations, then stop doing those things and don't surround yourself with people who bring you down.

For example, if your job gets you down and you cannot leave immediately, put a step-by-step plan together for what needs to be done. Start moving forward by looking for that dream job you have always wanted, update your résumé, and contact employment agencies. Doing so will give you a feeling of control that can give you the courage to make that job change.

Being calm is what life is all about.

Find a technique or different techniques that will calm you down and practice them daily. There are so many to choose from, so be sure to find something that fits well with you. But consider the following methods: Silva, yoga, mindfulness, or tai chi. Even if you have done some of these before, consider them again. Or why not try them in a different way like a walking meditation or listening to a different motivational speaker?

Live life here and now.

Whenever you get overwhelmed about a plan, focus on what needs to be done at the moment. Let's say you decide you want to run a marathon. When you start to feel intimidated by the amount of training involved, your physical limitations, or fitness, stop and think, *Right now I do not have to do that. Right now I just need to be able to walk around the block without getting all huffy and puffy.*

When you are overwhelmed with an intimidating project, stop and think about the immediate, small step that needs to be taken. Focus on the steps of the project that you can achieve now and have faith that you will be ready for each step as it arrives.

Journal your appreciation daily.

At the end of each day, list three or more things you are proud of or you have done well, which, in return, you can congratulate yourself for doing well. Practice giving yourself a pat on the back to strengthen the things you are proud of, and you will start to feel stronger and more capable.

Manage your destiny with a step-by-step plan.

Make the time to visualize what you want from life and start planning it all out to make this happen. Putting plans in place and working toward them is empowering. You will feel a sense of purpose and achievement when doing so. And yes, from time to time you will experience setbacks, but that is normal. When this happens, all you have to do is look over your plans and move on. Do not change your plans because of setbacks. Change your time frame or your pathway but never your destination.

What about the signs?

You know how sometimes we hear or say things like "I wonder if this is a sign from the Universe that I should not be doing this"? Hmmm … But all we do is wonder more when we are already in self-doubt. For example, if you are driving home and suddenly get a flat tire, are you to start thinking it is a sign that you should go somewhere else instead? No. You arrange to change the tire, but your destination is still the same. If you are shopping for dinner ingredients and the grocery store is out of stock of a certain item, you do not start wondering if it is a sign indicating you should skip that meal. No, of course not. You simply change your plans and make something else.

It is the same with life. You can rearrange even if you have low self-esteem. You do not need high self-esteem to take action. All you need is to start dreaming of the life you want to lead. Start dreaming and planning for the great things you are going to achieve. Dream big alongside planning, and take action. You and I know that we can achieve all we want. So give yourself the benefits that you deserve as well.

What are you going to do to make a change for the better?

Affirmation

- With all of my shortcomings, I still believe I am the best I can be.

PATHWAY 39

Keep It Moving by Just Starting

*Start by doing what's necessary; then do what's impossible;
and suddenly you are doing the impossible.*

—Francis of Assisi

Things to Do Before Starting Your Day

You do not have to be a morning person to benefit from morning routines. Most of the time people hit the snooze button once or twice before rolling out of bed and into some clothes to start the day without even having a plan in mind. On the other hand, you can decide to begin your day mindfully. Being mindful will increase the probability that you will feel good, be more productive, and end up happier when the day is over and done with.

Ideas that you can put into your morning routine, so your day can be a productive one:

Meditating daily can make your day easier to manage.

Meditating and/or simple breathing techniques can help you begin your day with a sense of calm. Instead of reaching for your smartphone or computer first thing in the morning, take a few minutes to sit and experience the quiet of peace that is within your house. There are lots of things to do during the day, so make a commitment to yourself to start your day on a quieter, kinder note. It will start the movement for your day and will help increase your focus, energy, and hope.

Gratitude is to be kept in mind.

Start your day by recalling what you are grateful for. A consistent habit of gratitude in the mornings will improve your awareness of it throughout your whole day. It will also make you stronger when challenges come your way and help you put your emotions into perspective.

Daily intention is a must.

Upon waking up first thing in the morning and before you start your day, meaning before getting out of bed, plan your day out by focusing on three goals you want to achieve that day. Make those goals a priority. When you set about planning your day with intention, you are more likely to feel productive at the end of your day.

If for some reason you were not able to complete the goals for the day, then you must start with that first thing the next morning before starting the goals for that day. So always do your best to complete your set goals for each day; that way, it will be easier for you to go with the flow of life. And if for some reason three goals are too many for one day, then set two or even one instead. The idea here is to achieve at least one goal daily in order to reach the main goal as planned.

Pace yourself throughout the day.

As you go about setting your daily goals, remember to pace your day and allow yourself space between goals. In other words, pacing your day with free time in between activities will give you a better chance of achieving your goals, which may even give you a break throughout the week.

Always keep hydrated.

Enjoy a glass of water first thing in the morning. It is suggested you drink half of your entire daily water intake by midmorning. It will flush your system of toxins, leave you feeling less hungry, and reduce headaches throughout the day. Plus, your energy level will increase. So, do yourself a favor and hydrate your body as needed; that way you are able to function at a higher level of mind.

Stretching your body will help you mentally.

It is not always easy to include exercise into your morning routine. Yet stretching your body first thing in the morning should be considered part of your daily routine. Consider adding a fifteen-minute muscle-stretching sequence of exercises to your morning schedule. It is a known fact that a regular routine stretching in the morning can increase flexibility, improve circulation, reduce stress throughout your day, and improve posture.

Music is a great way to start your day.

Starting your day with upbeat and fun music will not only wake you up but will fill you with positive energy for the whole day. It is a known fact that music makes you feel good. The two benefits of listening to music are mood regulation and self-awareness. Not only has it been shown to improve your mood, but it can end up increasing motivation, enhancing performance, and leading to better sleep at night.

Smile. Life is good.

First thing in the morning, start your day by smiling at yourself in the bathroom mirror. Smiling will have a positive effect on your overall attitude and well-being, even if you force it out of yourself. Smiling makes you friendlier, which will make you look trustworthy. In fact, it has been discovered that smiling will also make you a more effective leader. So be the leader of your life and smile daily.

Take care of and clean up after yourself.

Life is busy, and morning routines can be rushed. It can be very tempting when you are running behind to leave your clothes on the floor, dishes in the sink, and trash on the counter. Instead, just do it and get it over and done with. You do not want to come home having to clean a house after a long day's work. Plus, procrastination of cleaning up after yourself can prevent you from realizing your highest potential and best work. Believe it or not, it does hold truth. It also allows you to relax completely upon returning home from work. Therefore, it is better to proactively clean up after yourself than wait to be told.

Start with the hardest task first.

It might seem a little tempting to get a bunch of easy things checked off your to-do list, but it has been shown time and time again that doing your hardest task first leads to a more productive, easier, and happier day. You are more likely to remember the day as being a good one; therefore, your day will be better and easier to complete.

Doing the hardest first will help you stop procrastinating over the things you like to do the least. What will you do first thing in the morning to make your day a productive one?

Affirmation

- I may not always want to start something, but I always find the way to finish.

PATHWAY 40

Starting Each Day

It feels great to feel on top of the world but the greatest
feeling is when your feet are on the ground.
—Felix Baumgartner

Feeling on Top of the World

When you wake up in the morning, you are always asking yourself
questions whether you realize it or not. As you brush your teeth, as
you drink your tea or coffee, or as you eat breakfast, thoughts are
running through your mind nonstop. You might be thinking, *Why
am I so I tired today? Oh, why didn't I go to sleep earlier? What am
I going to make for breakfast?* Doing this normally does not do you
any good, and in some cases, as you can see, it might not even do
you justice at all.

The idea behind using questions first thing in the morning is to take
conscious control of the direction of your day.

Start Your Day by Asking Yourself the Following:

- What is my plan for the day?
- What is perfect about today?
- What is the best thing that could happen today?
- How can I make today totally successful and productive?

By asking yourself questions, you start to shift the focus of your mind toward all the things you want to do for the day and what needs to be done and how to achieve it. One thing to note is that your questions do not need to have any basis in reality because your brain will answer anything you ask it literally. So, if you are going to be delusional, you might as well make them extremely empowering.

The key to this is to use it consistently for thirty days in a row. What happens is that your brain will create a connection between the empowering solutions you create with your questions and being awake in the morning.

One Important Question to Include in Your Morning Routine

What am I grateful for? It is a known fact that you should start every single day with an attitude of gratitude. This is probably the simplest way to achieve that. If you ask yourself that question enough days in a row, you will wake up feeling on top of the world every single day. And as you start to view your life and the world around you as full of things to be grateful for, you are going to bring more of that into your life. We all have a lot to be grateful for, but we often get caught up in all the things that are wrong with our lives. Hopefully, this will allow you to shift your focus from now on.

Change Your Morning Routine Often

Think about changing the way you start your day. Consider being in a more peaceful and quiet way than you have in the past so as to set the pace for the rest of the day. You may find it quite powerful, and it will affect you physically and mentally. In other words, change your routine first thing in the morning.

Keep the Computer or TV Off

Many begin the day by turning on the television and computer. Starting your brain with such an overload immediately upon awakening cannot possibly be healthy for you. Just enjoy your tea or breakfast for about half an hour first.

Turning on the television is one of the most negative things you can do. The news can have such a negative impact on you that you might not even notice it. The news is mostly about everything that is going wrong in the world, and this is the first thing you become exposed to in the morning.

One thing that we know from years of self-help teaching is that our minds tend to be much more receptive in the mornings. Consider listening to music or something uplifting or inspiring. One of the best times to listen to a self-help CD is right when you wake up. Think about the positive effects it will have on you if you do this for thirty days in a row, fifteen minutes each time. You will condition your mind and connect it to waking up in the mornings, which will make it a lot easier for you.

Meditating Is the Solution to Everything

One of the most challenging things people face about meditating is to free themselves from their thoughts and fears. At times, we make meditation hard to understand and follow. Therefore, why not meditate when you are just waking up in the morning? That is when your mind is in a quiet state, so take fifteen minutes of your morning and do some deep-centered relaxation. Doing so can make your day a blissful one.

So ask yourself, how will you start your morning routine from now on?

Affirmation

- I begin each day with healthy morning routines that set the tone for a more productive day.

PATHWAY 41

How to Find Peace of Mind

All the flowers of all the tomorrows are in the seeds of today.

—Proverb

Practice and patience are attached like inseparable twins that have the potential to bring us great joy when they are balanced and great anxiety when they are not.

Consider this: Practice, and all comes in due time.

Diana: I did not realize the depth of this statement when I first heard it in one of my father's classes. This was said repeatedly to all who attended. And it is perfectly reasonable for one to assume he was referring to the daily practice of the Method and the timing that it takes to achieve a goal. But one morning while writing in my journal, I realized the true essence of his statement.

For as long as I can remember, I have attempted to know peace within—that is, peace while living in the real world and freedom from my cluttered mind. We all want that, do we not? And I am guessing that we all have some idea, whether through books or people, of how we are supposed to achieve this—self-awareness; detachment; letting go of failure, hurt, and pain; being present; etc.

Despite being aware of what we need to do, why do we often fail to do them? Why are we all not at peace? At times we might achieve lesser amounts of peace and happiness, and I believe as we experience life we get better, but why should this be the case if we know now what we are supposed to be doing?

So here is the understanding, in all its simplicity.

Practice and patience—even peace of mind comes with daily practice and patience. Just realizing this will improve your daily state of mind, regardless of how old you are. We do not need to think hard for ideas about how to understand what we need to do in improving. In other words, to become a great chef, you must practice cooking; a chef must master his recipes. The same applies to athletes: they must dedicate their lives to their sports, just as singers must exercise their voices. The same holds true with what goes on in our heads.

We must constantly remind ourselves to let go of the pain, hurt, failure, or whatever it might be that is causing distress and cluttering our minds. I say identify, solve, and let go daily and throughout the day, but this needs to be done repeatedly. This is what I now do every day and even more often when I am stressed, sad, or frustrated.

Let these random thoughts pass, and if something needs to be done, do it. Otherwise, plan when you will get it done and deal with it at the proper time. Then let it go. Let go of the thought and also the result and expectation tied to it. Do this with everything that causes you stress, never punish yourself when you find yourself struggling with the process, and always keep in mind to be patient with yourself and the process that it takes to achieve the outcome. I know and understand it is hard to be patient, but we can get better over time with practice.

Therefore, practice finding peace of mind daily and have patience with it—all comes in due time and in its proper timing.

Affirmation

- Every day I practice being patient by recognizing my thoughts and changing them when I feel out of sorts.

PATHWAY 42

Quieting Your Mind

You can learn to quiet your mind and
listen to the song of your soul.

—Katrina Mayer

A Quiet Mind

At this point in life, can you actually say you feel at peace with life? Are you a happy-go-lucky person with great joy and perfect happiness, free from problems and pain?

You might be one among the many who is aiming for a better life, wanting a peaceful and happy lifestyle. Yet it seems like an impossible thing to accomplish—where we end up mentally belittling ourselves for not achieving, therefore lacking peace of mind.

We need to understand that it is not our true state. We get so caught up being distracted with the fast pace of life that we momentarily lose touch with our natural states of being.

Here is a technique that will bring positive feelings into your life:

197

Find the peace and happiness that is within you.

To correct problems, you must first acknowledge them. Then understand that problems, most of the time, are created and started within the mind. The same pattern happens many times; therefore, some external event takes place within the mind. However, we then choose to see only one side of the story and then interpret the situation as such that it causes us some kind of mental struggle, ending in some kind of emotional suffering.

It is easy to say, "Let go of your problems," and yet many of us know it is not quite that simple. We have all had many years of negative conditioning, attracting problems and conflicts. Therefore, the concept of *letting go of your problems* will not be as effective as it was before. That is the reason for self-help techniques and tools that help bring solutions and success into our daily routines.

Close your eyes for about a minute or so … Really take the time to do it, and during this time, tell yourself that you want silence and stillness and try to avoid chattering negative thoughts. You might notice that the moment you become silent, thoughts start coming to mind unexpectedly, and you might even get thoughts that have no relation to anything that is happening to you at the moment. This is what we call *distracting thoughts*, which pull us away from our inner silence. And this, my friend, was only a simple test where we consciously observed our minds and did our best to become still but probably could not yet achieve it.

As a result, the space that is within us becomes cluttered with useless negative thoughts that do not bring goodness to our well-being. And because our space is cluttered, our inner clarity and wisdom become distant and unclear. Therefore, we lose touch with that part of our inner selves that is pure, peaceful, wise, and eternal.

The many things we find important in our lives, such as watching television, updating our Facebook and Twitter accounts, checking email, and the like, can make us go in many different directions. Therefore, our attention will be distracted and taken away from the things that are truly important to us—the things that will bring lasting happiness and fulfillment to our lives and the lives of those we encounter.

Whether we recognize it or not, the information perceived is to bring ourselves to our inner space to some level, which does affect our emotions and desires. If we are not careful about it, we can easily rush through life while focusing on the things that have no meaning to us and then wonder, *Where did my life go? Why do I feel so unhappy and unfulfilled?*

If you are alive, eating, breathing, and living right now, then you have been given another day to live. Wake up and take control of your future, which is your passion, and start living it soon, regardless of your age.

Mental Housecleaning is a must.

One way to clear out the mental clutter is by protecting your mind from it. We should be conscious of what we allow inside, starting with our own words, thoughts, and actions because what we say, think, and do really does affect us.

Keep in mind that we may not be aware that this is happening. Think about it; we spend so much energy judging and finding fault with others, not realizing we have spent so much time consuming ourselves in negative thoughts, such as jealousy, guilt, or fear, while making up excuses to cover up how we *really* feel. This may sound exaggerated, but if we truly see ourselves with open minds, we notice that our thoughts and words, at some point during the day, quietly and/or unconsciously are doing these things. It is okay to do so, as long as you take notice of it and change it for the better.

Sometimes an action is unnoticed, such as expressing a negative judgment toward a waiter, becoming frustrated with a telephone customer service representative and wanting to tell them off, or lying to get out of a commitment when all you really needed to say was *no.*

These thoughts and actions do not define anyone as bad. They are merely negative thoughts that clutter our inner minds and affect our well-being.

Rules to Mental Housecleaning

Say what you mean. Mean what you say.
Do not say to anyone unless you can say to everyone.
Do not say inside what you cannot say outside.
Do not say unless it is true, useful, or kind.

Use the rules above to quiet the mind.

Say what you mean. Mean what you say.

Say what you mean.

Are you making up excuses to avoid meeting up with someone you are not comfortable meeting up with? For example, your friend invites you to a fun event. You do not really want to go, so you make up an excuse and tell her, "I cannot go," or, "I am so busy today," which might work. That is a fast way to avoid something or someone or maybe even a gathering you really did not want to go to in the first place.

Another example: Someone asked you for a favor, and you really do not feel like helping out, but you feel guilty saying no. So, instead, you either avoid that person and/or ignore his or her phone calls. For example, you say, "I am out of town," when you really are at home relaxing. It is not that you cannot go; it is that you have chosen not to go or do something about it. But creating an excuse or avoiding it completely creates a chatter in your inner mind, and that itself takes a lot of energy to maintain. So instead of having stillness and peace, you now have thoughts about that story lingering in your mind.

When you are about to speak, make a conscious decision to say what holds true and/or what you actually mean. The absolute truth does not have to be harsh or hurtful. You can express it compassionately and lovingly yet firmly at the same time. When you own what you say, no one can reject it, even if that person does not like what he or she hears—only because you are telling the truth and you mean it with a loving heart.

Mean what you say.

There are many times when we commit to things out of habit or obligation that we had no intention of following through with. For example, we say, "I love you," to our parents or our better halves when we are done speaking to them on the phone, not because we mean it but out of habit. Those words are usually said automatically, and then they start to lose their true meaning and value.

Another example would be when we say, "I will call you soon." Yet we have no intention of following through. We may think that these moments are innocent, but they become the little made-up stories that we materialize mentally, and over time, they will develop into a guilty conscience. What you need to do is make a conscious commitment to yourself to mean everything you say and not make empty promises you cannot and will not fulfill.

Do not say to anyone unless you can say to everyone.

Whether we like to admit it or not, at one point or another, we gossip about each other. We are so quick to find fault in others, and then we turn around to talk about them with our best friends or talk about someone else's troubles. We can all relate to this.

Jenny, a coworker, had an emotional fit and yelled at another coworker today, and when Judy got home, she immediately told her loved ones about the drama that took place at work.

Another example: Rosie was fired from her job, and once we heard about it, we called or texted our friend Wilma to tell her about it and exchange jokes about Rosie, just because she is not very well liked.

When we consciously take notice of what is happening, we notice that we are not learning positive and good ways of living. Nothing positive comes from it. Instead, we create pure drama and negative energy that causes inner conflict, cluttering our inner space.

Make a commitment to yourself now that you will not say something to anyone unless you can announce it to the world—meaning to everyone. Make a commitment now to stop the spreading of negative drama and energy.

Do not say inside what you cannot say outside.

Most of us are extremely critical about ourselves. We would never tell the world what we say to ourselves in the privacy of our minds. We believe that we are the only ones affected by negative self-talk, low self-esteem, and anxiety, but we are not.

When something does not go our way, we are the first to blame ourselves, criticizing what we did wrong, belittling ourselves at times to the point of no return, and all because of what we missed.

We need to keep in mind that we all have mental inner chatter, but problems come up when we start to believe in the chattering. Then we start to create false beliefs about ourselves. These false beliefs become harmful to our spirits and future well-being unless we do something to unlearn these beliefs or change them to better our lives.

Next time, when you hear yourself saying, "I am stupid," "I am not good enough," "I am such a failure," and so on, recognize that it is not you. Therefore, you can say, "That is not me—that statement holds no truth."

Say the following affirmation: "I choose to let go of the negative thoughts that hold me back from who I truly am."

The basic third rule to mental housecleaning is that whatever thought you are not able to say out loud to everyone, or anyone, for that matter, is not allowed to linger inside your head.

Do not say unless it is true, useful, or kind.

Some people have so much mental clutter that it comes out in useless talk. Take notice of people who talk on the subway or the ones who love to chitchat at work by the break room. If you can, pay attention to how many things they say are actually useful and/or interesting. It will likely not be many.

Not only is this distracting for those around this kind of person, but it also takes a lot of energy for them to keep talking to this person. Just bring back to mind the last time you talked for a long time about something out of nowhere and how it drained you completely. Therefore, the less we say negative, useless things to ourselves, the better our minds will be. If this is you, do not allow it to let you down. You are not alone. Many others have been there too, yet it is possible to quiet the mind.

Some people practice going through sabbatical days when they do not speak, read, or use their computers and smartphones. When doing so, they feel a huge sense of peace, happiness, and positive energy building up inside them. Try it out for yourself. You never know what improvements can come from practicing sabbatical.

Be conscious of what you say, and only say it if it holds true.

Is what I am saying holding truth to me. For example, a true fact always comes from the heart. Being useful and/or helpful to someone or some situation also comes from the heart if it is true. Being kind and/or compassionate to everyone will always be in your favor. Giving a compliment or offering your help is a blissful feeling in return.

If you can answer these questions, you can find a way to better, positive, constructive thoughts that can lead you to a better life.

Quieting the Mind

It may look difficult at first, but if you follow it consistently and consciously for at least seven days, it becomes easier. Then you can extend it to fourteen days and then to twenty-one days, and before you know it, you have completed the thirty days. Never judge yourself or give up just because you forget the rules—which happens to everyone. Let it go and continue moving forward nicely. And as time goes on, notice how your outer world changes as your inner world is being transformed into a better lifestyle. By doing so, your heart will always guide you to your passion. Learn to trust and listen to your heart, for it always knows what is best for you.

Affirmations

- I no longer gossip about anyone.
- I mean what I say and say what I mean.
- By meditating, I keep my mind still and serene.

Discovering Your Passion

It's your place in the world; it's your life. Go on and do all
you can with it, and make it the life you want to live.
—Mae Jemison

Following the Passion You Have Always Dreamed Of

Diana: Recently, I woke up earlier than expected, and as I was there, I started thinking about my life and how is it that I got myself living someone else's life. The house is usually quiet until about ten o'clock in the morning. Because of this, early mornings were the perfect time to think and meditate for a purpose.

I started thinking that as a child, I knew exactly what I wanted to be and do. I wanted to be a motivational presenter, a self-help coach, and an author who wrote a book about how to help others in times of need. And as an adult, for a moment, those dreams became distant. That happened to me because I listened to everyone else around me, and they all knew what I wanted—so they thought. They all knew what I needed to do, and that was to go to college, get a steady job, get married, buy a house, have many children, and work hard until retirement.

I would listen to everyone else and did my best to fit myself into something that was not who I was. I went from one job to another, feeling stressed out about it, and each time ending up further away from my dreams. The only thing that kept me away from my goals and dreams was me.

The Fear of Trying

Have you ever had a feeling that comes from deep down within your heart that what you are doing is not working for you, but you are too afraid to try something new? I went from one job to another, doing my best to do away with the dread that I felt each morning as I got ready for work because none of the jobs I had were working for me. Nothing gave me the spark that made me feel truly alive. Because I spend most of my time at work, I thought it should be something I love and enjoy doing daily.

I was dealing with compliance calls, and that was something I should have adapted to quickly, but some of us cannot. I knew that I should have achieved because everyone I worked with seemed to be doing well but me.

Sometimes you spend so much time listening to everyone else that you forget what your voice even sounds like. This leads to forgetting who you are and who you want to be. I was so out of sync with myself that I did not know where to start because I did what I was supposed to do. I had followed the formula that everyone does, but I was still not happy with that.

Starting Over Can Be Exciting

I finally took the step forward to start a whole new life. For me, this was the perfect time to start again. I began writing a book that I had started many months earlier but had never finished. I also became a life coach for the Silva Method, which brings me lots of success in many areas of my life. I also began recording videos of myself.

I cannot say that everything has been okay from the start because I made lots of mistakes. I was not good at time management. I have had lots of struggles finding a job, which made it hard to stay motivated when times were tough, but that is what life is all about.

Yet we are so ready to share the information about the obstacles we have faced, how great our lives are now, and how others can achieve it too, but rarely do we mention the struggle it took to get to that point.

That usually happens because it is hard to let go of what you know to try something new; even if you knew that it was not working for you, there is still a part of you that wants to hang onto it only because it is hard to break away from old habits. I understand that it is hard to follow a new path and find a new way. Know that you will stumble a lot along the way. I am not telling you this to discourage you. I am telling you this to prepare yourself for an incredible adventure that lies ahead of you.

Success Comes from Hard Work

I have experienced unbelievable lows and highs in my life. There were many times when I felt I was not going to make it through, and yet, at the same time, I was able to experience lots of amazing highs that I did not even see coming. I would have never known them if I was not willing to take that first step into the unknown to start doing what I love instead of what I thought I was supposed to do. Hard work does bring great rewards in return. Now I wake up feeling so excited about what the day will bring because I love my job.

Now that you know what needs to be done, let us look at the first step. Before you can begin to do what you are passionate about for a living, you need to figure out what exactly your passion is. Many people do not really know what their passions are because it has been so long since they have been in touch with themselves. That is nothing to be ashamed about because it happens to all of us at one time or another.

Below are some questions you can use to get in touch with your passion:

What are your traits?

Everyone is good at something or has a talent that he or she is good at. If you cannot think of one right away, do your best to think back to when people in your life gave you compliments for doing so well. Do people regularly compliment you on who you are or what you do? Do they think you have what it takes to be a motivational speaker? Are you good at making others feel comfortable and loved? Are you a good listener who has lots of advice to share? Are you an energetic person who loves to help others stay healthy? Are you good with animals that need to be rescued? What is it that you are good at? There is something out there that you are passionate about!

How do you spend your free time?

How do you spend your time when you have completed your day? What do you look forward to after you are done with your daily routine? Most of the time you will find that what you do in your free time reveals what you are already good at. Therefore, finding your passion should be easier.

What were your childhood hobbies?

If nothing comes to mind for what you are good at, try looking back at your childhood memories for ideas. What did you want to be when you grew up? How did that make you feel?

I myself want to be a writer and a life coach at the same time because the act of helping others made me feel complete. Maybe you wanted to be a teacher because you wanted to help people learn how to read, write, and talk, and that would be wonderful.

I realized that looking back to my childhood joys guided me to what I really wanted to do with my life, and I bet you can find yours too.

What if everything was guaranteed?

How would you spend your time? What would you do that would engage your mind?

You will probably ask yourself these questions and come up with a bunch of ideas that you think are no good at all. You can figure out ways to combine your skills with the work you already do. Knowing your strengths and using them to your advantage will make you a better person.

If you are an ambitious person, you might want to do things a little differently. For example, if the job you want does not exist, then it is up to you to create it. The internet is full of examples of people who took the ideas they were most passionate about and turned them into lifetime careers. You can do this, and all you have to do is get out of your comfort zone. Take a few minutes every day to brainstorm ways you can get paid to do what you are passionate about. You will never solve the problem if you do not take the time to think up a solution while doing mental housecleaning. Then go after some of those ideas by doing work on the side to figure out what might work for you.

The only limit to what is possible for you is the limit you put on yourself. I am not here to tell you how big your dreams should be. That would be up to you. So dream big or dream small, whichever you chose is your choice.

Everyone you meet is different from the others, and every dream, no matter the size of the dream, is needed. And that is because everything we do as a living is considered to be humanitarian, which helps make the world complete. So, learn to let go of the fear that holds you back and do away from the worries of insecurity and self-doubt by committing yourself to doing something you love. Anything and everything you do in this world is considered to be humanitarian. We are here to help each other move forward through life in a successful and fruitful way. Life is too short. The sooner you begin, the sooner you will see the possibilities and start to live them daily.

Affirmation

- I meditate on what really excites me, and I give my all to everything I do.

PATHWAY 44

Learning Positive Ways for Any Situation

Every situation is a positive situation if viewed as
an opportunity for growth and self-mastery.

—Brian Tracy

The power of staying positive, whatever the situation, can never be underestimated. Because we are all here for a limited period of time, is it worth it to spend any of that time in a negative mood? No!

The true test of anyone to remain positive is when challenges become difficult. Remaining positive keeps one's mind in the right state of balance and often opens solutions to the problems at hand. Negativity is contagious; not only does it affect us, but it also affects everyone we come in contact with. When only the negative situation is in focus, the solution process becomes blocked.

Being positive is a mindset that can be present at any moment, and it can turn into a good habit. Here are some tips that can help you shift your mindset.

Shifting Your Thoughts Can Be a Lifesaver

Be conscious of your thoughts more so when life is not going your way. Shift your thoughts the moment you see yourself diving into agony, frustration, sorrow, and low self-esteem by thinking about something positive. By doing so, it will break the pattern of self-pity, mind-created stories, and negative thoughts becoming out of control. What makes us different from others is our ability to control our thoughts and think for ourselves.

Find the Lesson in All That You Learn

There is a lesson to be learned from every situation. No matter how difficult the situation may appear, accept and acknowledge the beautiful lessons waiting to be discovered. Sometimes lessons are of great value, but every problem is a learning opportunity in disguise. You may have made a mistake or two, but now you can accept them and continue moving forward, knowing that you will make a different decision in the future. Understand and appreciate what you have learned from the experience.

The Attitude of Gratitude Will Always Be the Solution

You cannot be angry and grateful at the same time. Count all the blessings and miracles in your life. Start looking for them, and when doing so, you tend to find more. What is there not to be grateful for? Are you not alive and breathing? Of course you are! Therefore, realize how lucky you are to have all the abundance you have at the moment.

Positive Visualization and Affirmations

For visualization, practice seeing yourself positive, confident, and knowledgeable. Do this whenever you find yourself with some spare time—for example, while sitting on the bus, waiting for a friend, or taking the elevator. For self-affirmations, listing positive statements about yourself and your self-image is a powerful tool to use. It trains your subconscious to see yourself in a positive way. This is important, as many of us can be so hard on ourselves because of social conditioning.

Memories Can Make Life Beautiful

Keep a journal of memories that can quickly make you smile. Fill it with memorable occasions when you felt happy, appreciative, and hopeful and when you were at peace with the world. Whenever you find yourself in a negative state of mind, consciously and deliberately pick any memory out of this list and dwell on it. Reminiscing about those happy moments gives a balanced perspective to your situation. You realize that what looks negative today will change tomorrow. Nothing stays the same. Nothing will last forever.

Criticizing Others for Their Choices

Changing your attitude and the way you see life can be the great blessing of all. See if you can stop criticizing others and situations. Our culture teaches us to find flaws and problems at all times. Shifting the way you see life and everything around you, from flaws to appreciation, can bring you endless blessings in life. Whether you are positive or negative, the situation does not change if you do not make it happen, so it might as well be positive instead.

As with any habit, the habit of staying positive in all situations takes practice and a commitment to yourself to take control. To start, one needs to take small steps while giving attention to your emotions. But first, one needs to start by wanting to change. Keep going at it, and you will progressively become a positive energy source to everyone around you. Wow! That is so empowering.

Affirmations

- When a negative thought surfaces, I allow myself to express the thought and then change it to a positive thought that leads to a much-desired outcome.
- When I hear another expressing a negative thought, I remind myself that person is on a different path, and I can alter the thought in my mind to avoid negativity.

PATHWAY 45

Manifesting Positive Thoughts through Self-Talking

Your self-talk is the channel of behavior change.
—Gino Norris

Avoid Negative Self-Talk Statements

Do you know what makes life challenging? It is us and our brains that always look for drama, repeating negative self-talk and creating false images of fear, which, in turn, make our lives difficult in every area. Every struggle we go through daily, which includes every disagreement, dissatisfaction, and problem, can come down to a single cause that our brains tell us nonstop.

It is the brain's responsibility to keep us safe from any situation, yet it is constantly acting from a place of fear. The brain's job is to ensure our survival. And in doing so, its job is not to guarantee that we have joyful experiences while we are living. Even when everything is going

215

so well, a little voice inside our heads will say, "Be careful. Something unforeseen might happen." And once that is said, panic sets in, and we experience that discouraging, anxious feeling of possibly losing all the good we have going for us at the moment.

The brain is always ready to tell us interesting yet terrifying stories that are so convincing they will influence us to also act out of fear due to silly anxieties that take place. But not only that, the brain will vividly repeat the emotional stories on our mental screens over and over again, like it is a dress rehearsal to an endless song. This is self-mental abuse because we sabotage ourselves to no end. And before you know it, you will start to believe in the story and trust it to be true. It becomes so embedded in your mind in the form of a belief even if it is not true. We then continue our life's journey and take action from a place that is a negative and false belief.

The problem with that is we end up suffering. Many times we suffer a lot, and sometimes we suffer for a long period of time. We suffer because we do not realize that we are the problem, and yet, at the same time, we are the solution.

Negative Self-Talk That Takes Over Constantly

Diana: For the past few years, I have been carrying with me a repeating thought, and to some point, it has become somewhat of a heavy belief that I am not as good of a mother as I should be. Like many of our self-defeating thoughts, it whispers quietly in our ears, and its negative energy spreads like a vicious virus. We realize that it is there, but because it is difficult to separate it from reality, we allow it to stay because the brain has a voice of its own, and it feels real and true.

In the example I am about to share, I had believed it was true; therefore, I bought into the story. Feeling completely incompetent as a parent, I did what I could to stay busy at work and to trust that my baby boy was safe. At that time, it was heartbreaking for me. I kept this secret silently tucked away in the privacy of my mind, and now I will share it with you after so many years of mental torment.

No one saw what I was going through at that moment. Everyone at work saw that I was focused on my employment; after all, lots of children are taken to a day care center at a very young age. But within my heart, I was crying. I would keep myself busy at work because the thought of my son being in a day care center scared me deeply.

My son at the age of eight months was abused by a babysitter I had hired from my sister. The abuse happened two months after I hired her. I will never forget the cry my son made when he saw me when I returned from work, and I will never forgive myself for not realizing what was happening sooner. I enrolled him in a day care center, but the more I stayed away and focused on work, the worse I felt. I deemed myself a bad mother and mentally tortured myself.

This kind of a situation can bring you down fast if you allow it to. In these private mental negative wars, we battle where nobody wins, and we feel like we are in a constant bad dream.

Looking at my precious baby boy, now a young man, radiating life and so full of joy and love, I feel a surge of emotions. I have mixed feelings of guilt for having missed what a mother should have done to protect her child. I put my forehead against his forehead, his dark brown eyes looking straight into my soul, and I gently whispered, "I love you, sweetie." I tell myself that I will always enjoy every moment with him and protect him as much as I can.

So, I took him out of the day care center and decided to work on my schedule so I can be a full-time mother again. No more drama to his life or mine. No more mental lies or self-abuse. I got another chance at this important job as a mother without illusions and without guilt.

I wanted to be there fully for my son, going through his ups and downs—but mostly when he needs me.

I do not think these thoughts will ever go away, which is ironic given that I am writing on how to stop manifesting negative thoughts. While we cannot completely stop the negative self-talk, we can work toward a new reality where we stop believing in all that is happening. We can do our best to practice awareness in recognizing when these thoughts are happening and choose not to buy into the abuse we inflict on ourselves on a daily basis. Instead, we can say, "Thank you for sharing," or cancel the negative thought and replace it with a positive thought.

What unsupported thoughts are you hearing in your mind repeatedly? What self-defeating, abusive, and limiting negative statement is your brain trying to convince you of or has convinced you to hold true?

Take a minute to reflect on what you are worried, stressed, or anxious about recently. What thoughts have been running repeatedly in your head? Make a list and notice what is happening and then be aware that it is there in order for it to be known. When we are facing the light that shines on our future, the shadows must fall behind us in order to keep moving forward successfully.

Common Negative Thoughts That Might Hold You Back

I am …

- Not a good enough person
- Ugly to the eyes of others
- Too fat, tall, short, young, or old
- Not deserving
- Not capable of anything

- Not as smart as I would like to be
- Not as lovable
- Such a bad parent
- Such a horrible person

I will never be loved.

There is something wrong with me inside and out.

All of these are illusions created by the mind, which will limit our capacity to fully enjoy life. Therefore, when we get lost in the story, we miss the gifts that are meant for us at the moment. This moment, after all, is all we have. Once we lose it, it is gone forever. Let us always do our best to enjoy it to the fullest while we can.

Affirmation

- When I start to engage in negative self-talk, I quiet my mind and replace it with positive statements.

PATHWAY 46

Focusing on What You Want

It's all in the mind.

—George Harrison

Train Yourself to Meditate with Shapes and Color

There can be many reasons we do not always get what we want in life. One of these reasons is because we focus on the opposite of what we really want, and many times, we just cannot help it. But if we are conscious of our thoughts, we can take them and shift our frame of mind toward our desired goals.

Think about a time you were bothered by a person or situation. The more we complain about it, the more we notice it. And the more we notice it, the worse it becomes and the next time we interact with that person or situation, we expect to be annoyed all over again. We are unconsciously looking for those small triggers that will make us annoyed.

For example, have you ever shopped for a certain type of car that you have never noticed before? A black Cadillac or a gold BMW, for example, and then, suddenly, you see them everywhere? Or have you bought a creamy silk blouse with peach pearl on the trimmings, and suddenly you notice them everywhere in the stores?

Whether we focus on things we want or do not want, we get whatever we focus on.

Here is a simple exercise to follow:

Before you say anything, do this simple yet powerful exercise that can be done anywhere.

Close your eyes, take three deep breaths, pick any shape, and focus on it with color. Look for that kind of shape and color on your mental screen while moving forward with the day. For example, focus on finding a big, red circle-shaped object. Now, bring that shape and color into mind. Do this for several minutes. Do you now notice more red circle-shaped objects?

Now, pick another shape and color and focus on that. Forget about the red circle shape, just focus on the second shape. Focus only on green square-shaped objects.

Continue doing this for several minutes. Remember to scan your surroundings mentally. Do you suddenly notice your second shape everywhere? Repeat the process several times using different shapes and colors each time.

I first learned about this wonderful technique from my father at a very young age. We were in the car, and I was not having a good day. He used this technique to remind me that focusing on thoughts of frustration will only make the frustrations stronger and bigger. I was so excited with what I had learned that day. I learned that we can take control and shift our thoughts by shifting our focus. A shift in our thoughts will shift our emotions right on the spot, but only if we allow them to.

Practicing in Real Life Makes Dreams Come True

Practicing daily and being persistent always find solutions. So, how can I put this into practice? There are many situations where you can benefit by putting your power of focus into practice. Meditating is a good start when practicing daily—a good, positive habit to put into your daily routine.

Some suggestions to be of help to you:

Find the good in those who annoy you.

It is without a doubt that we will interact, at one time or another, with people who frustrate us. And instead of focusing on why they frustrate us or why they bring us feelings of frustration, we should focus on the things we admire about them. It might take some time and practice to achieve but if at that moment, the person is in your presence, start as soon as you can. So look for things you like and admire about the person. Perhaps he or she is wearing something nice or has a classy hair style, or you admire the person's work values. The idea here is to focus on the good and positive things instead of the negative.

Frustrating situations—see the outcome.

When situations do not favor our expectations, it can be so frustrating. And the more we think about how annoyed we are, the more anger is consumed, which does not help the situation or your health. So instead, focus on the positive side of the situation and make an effort to focus only on that. I know this at times can be hard to achieve, but if you start today, it becomes easier. So, look for things that you learned and/or enjoyed about the situation.

For example, two years ago, I booked a flight from Houston, Texas, to Miami, Florida. What should have been a two-flight connection turned out to be four due to delays and transfers from one airplane to another, forcing me to run from one corner of the airport to the other for the next terminal. This was such a frustrating and stressful situation, yet I got to my destination safe and sound.

Do not complain about not feeling well.

When you physically do not feel well, do you notice that you like to tell yourself that you are not feeling well? We also like to take the opportunity to tell anyone and everyone that we feel sick. Yet we do not realize that we can get sick by simply saying, "I am sick," or, "I feel sick." While you are entitled to say anything you want, what will actually help you to get better is focusing on being healthy again. So when you are sick or saying you are sick, you should take time off to rest and allow your body to recover and, when doing so, focus on the image of yourself in perfect health. But keep in mind that for the shift to take place, you must stop saying or envisioning yourself as sick because, in due time, it will manifest. So always watch what you say, think, and do.

Find what is right with your job.

I have heard of this from others, and I have repeated it when the moments get really tough on me. Though the result is always the same, as I find more reasons to dislike my job, I feel even more dissatisfied. In these moments, I have a tendency to forget just how lucky and privileged I am to have such a job. My focus on the dislike of my job puts me into a negative downward spiral like it always does. So instead, start being picky and focus on the things you enjoy about your job and all the wonderful opportunities that come with it. Create a list in your journal of personal benefits from your job, and then focus on each point one by one. For example, financial security, time flexibility, creative expression, feeling of empowerment when completing a project, inspirational coworkers, learning from each other, chances to help others, health insurance, stock and shareholders' options, and the list goes on.

End jealousy.

When we find others better than what we think we are, it becomes easy to get caught up in feelings of jealousy, which is always self-destructive. Therefore, instead of focusing on why others are undeserving, learn from them and choose to understand what makes them worthy. Express highly what they have done well and reasons why they have been successful. Now use these insights as a source of inspiration to help yourself excel too, and never see it as competition. If you do, it will never end.

Make the delay work for you.

The problems with traveling can be frustrating experiences more so when leaving home, which takes us outside of our comfort zone. Focusing on how frustrating it is will only make us feel worse. So instead, focus on the qualities that are empowering about the experience.

How can you make the experience a positive one? For example, you can perhaps focus on having the extra few hours to catch up on your reading or making a new friend while waiting for your next connecting flight or being happy that you are alive and breathing and doing better than others or realizing that the flight delay is to ensure your safety. Therefore, you are thankful for that. The delay of your luggage is inconvenient, but at least they will deliver your bags to you for free so you do not have to wait at the airport for them. There is a lot that can be done without stressing yourself and/or your health.

There are not enough hours in the day.

Have you ever started a conversation like that? But then you wasted time on unproductive things such as browsing the internet, chatting with a friend on social media, or watching television. I have been there many times too. Most of the time it is an excuse to avoid doing something we do not want to do. Yet if something is important enough, we can create time to make it happen. Instead of saying you do not have enough time for whatever reason and then just brushing it off, practice asking yourself how you can create time to do this, make it a reality, or free up some time from your schedule.

Fear brings failure.

The more we focus on the object of our fear, the more powerful the feeling gets. Life rarely turns out as bad as we assume it to be. Focusing on the worst possible outcome is extremely stressful, takes a lot of energy to maintain, and brings you no success in life. Whether it is asking someone out on a date or giving a presentation to an audience, it does not help to say, "I am afraid," "I am going to fail," or "What if I look stupid? I might as well not even try." So instead, focus on what it is that you do want. Focus by repeating what you want in the present tense. For example: "I am confident and knowledgeable about this topic, and I can give an empowering presentation. It is a breeze, and I can do it all."

This can be applied to all situations in life or anything you encounter, including the following:

- getting a job
- losing weight
- finding a date
- waiting on the phone for a representative

We hope this simple skill of focus will add to your tools and techniques and that it will help you for years to come. Remember to stay faithful to your meditations in order to open new doors that are always waiting for you to enter.

Affirmation

- I use clear and colorful images while meditating on what it is I desire to achieve.

PATHWAY 47

The Power of Silence

Silence is the sleep that nourishes wisdom.

—Francis Bacon

What Silence Can Bring

Diana: I remember when I was a little child that as a family, we would take long road trips when we were out of school during summer break. We were from the lower part of Texas, so in order to get anywhere, the drive was at least four hours long. But being that we were an ambitious family, a four-hour drive was a weekend trip to my grandmother's house.

We loved visiting my grandmother, but sometimes, we would travel to Mexico City, which was a fourteen-hour drive. When you travel with more people than you can count in a car for that long, there will be issues along the way. I can vividly recall that one of those issues was the radio.

Because my father drove most of the time, we were at his mercy when it came to listening to the radio or, more often, not listening to the radio for the silence my father was seeking. My father would insist on turning off the radio every so often so that he can hear himself think—that is what he would say to us. So, we would whine and complain and say, "It is just so boring without listening to anything."

Now let us move forward decades later, and suddenly, I find myself turning off the music at home or while I am at work or even when I am driving. This is odd for me because I love music, and I usually do not go anywhere without listening to it.

I started to wonder what this was all about. Perhaps I am at the same age my father was when he was telling us he needed time to listen to his thoughts. But most likely I think it is that I have finally come to appreciate silence.

Silence and What Comes with It

Rest is not just about taking a nap or getting your eight hours of sleep every night. We have to keep in mind that our brains are constantly being bombarded with too much information, and the majority of it is a waste of time. For example, we have obligations at work, obligations at home, and obligations we maintain socially. Our minds are full of to-do lists, and when you add publicity and social media … wow! Talk about having an overloaded brain.

I, for one, can say that I am happy with all the relationships I have at work, at home, and with my friends. I never wish to do away with these relationships from my life, but sometimes my brain feels tired. So I start thinking to myself, *Who am I kidding?* Sometimes my whole body feels tired too. And what seems to be helping me is cutting back on my usage of the internet, which includes watching television and listening to music or any podcasts and/or videos. Instead, I just go outside to enjoy nature at its best.

But remember not to get discouraged when you do your best to rest because your mind might jump around from one thought to another with the silence it feels it needs to fill. That is exactly what happens to many. Eventually, it settles down, and when that happens, you rest. Therefore, you are able to enjoy the ability to focus fully on whatever task needs to be done for the day. Lately, I have been enjoying cooking in silence. When doing so, I can smell the aromas better, and the end result seems to taste so much better.

Now let's talk about multitasking, which can overwhelm our brains tremendously. For example, listening to the news while cooking a meal and completing other activities is a form of multitasking. I am not saying we must not multitask because, in one form or another, we all do it every day. What I am saying is that I do believe our brains could use a break now and then, so they can recharge for the next task. For me, meditating is a great way to rest the mind, body, and soul.

Give Yourself Time to Reflect

Just like a computer, our brains must reflect all the information we collect daily. And just like a computer, our brains slow down and struggle with the processing of things when we have too much running through our minds all at once.

In order to act from a place of love, we need to be able to understand and deal with what happens in our lives. We need to process the information we perceive and receive. I know for a fact that meditation works really well for this, but the choice is yours to make.

Many times, I find the easiest way for me to process is to go for a walk. I take my headphones in order to distract myself from the nonstop thinking, but one day I decided to go without the headphones and actually enjoyed it much better. Instead of feeling miserable the whole day, I ended up feeling better and more clear-minded.

And now every time I go for a walk I leave the headphones behind. It gives me time to deal with what happened in my day, which allows me to act instead of reacting. So, the next time you are looking for clarity, seek some silence and focus on a task that takes less thinking to do, such as going for a walk or taking pictures. I bet after a thirty-minute walk or whatever brings you clarity, you will feel better and more in tune to yourself and the world around you.

Get Comfortable with Silence

I can say that I was born with the natural ability to talk in a way that people find my chat useful. A few of my friends are the same way. So when we get together, we can talk for hours. But if we are around each other for too long, our conversations become shallow. For example, we start talking about ice cream for fifteen minutes while waiting in line at the grocery store. Not that it's a bad thing to do, but it can get a little silly and redundant.

I never realized this until I started spending time with a few people who were much quieter than I was—one of whom is a sister in Christ. I was doing all the talking, and these friends were not really responding. I was a little hurt at first, but then I thought about what I was saying and realized that there was not much left to respond with but dead air.

But when they made conversation, what they said was insightful, humorous, and thoughtful. I valued what they brought into my life because I learned that it is okay to be quiet around someone else. The conversations we have now are deeper, and I have learned to practice thinking before speaking, which, of course, helps.

But do not get me wrong. I still love getting on the phone to chat with my chatty friends, but I also value the moments of silence in between. I have found that even my chatty friends do not mind at all being quiet now that they know I enjoy silence.

When you are having nonstop conversations, give yourself the chance for some silence after every conversation you have with someone. These moments give you time to reflect on what you have heard or what you are about to say. It allows you to be a better friend, coworker, partner, and much more. There really is something to be said for the quality of what you share over the quantity.

In my experience and journey with silence, I feel like I have found a place of peace where love is always found. Plus, I have made tremendous positive changes in myself, including the world around me, just by being silent.

I encourage you to enjoy the silence when you allow it into your life while extending it, little by little, outside your comfort zone. The results will amaze you.

Affirmation

- I practice being comfortable with the idea of silence, allowing the following moments to happen as they may.

PATHWAY 48

Keeping Calm

Feeling overwhelmed is a sign you're not being true to yourself.
—Julia Reed

The Agony of Being Overwhelmed

Have you ever gotten yourself in a situation where you had multiple deadlines to meet, a long list of unfinished tasks to complete, and past-due bills to pay? And still family, friends, and your boss were asking you to do more? What can we do to gain back control of these uncontrolled, stressful situations?

We live in a world that has become busier than ever before. Things are moving at a much faster pace, and we are forced to move right along with the motions of the pace. And because of that, more is required out of an average person than ever before. Yet the benefit to our fast-moving society is that we are able to receive much more than our grandparents would have ever imagined possible. But the only thing is that we are often overwhelmed by the number of things we are responsible for and that are required of us.

Many times, the feeling of being overwhelmed does not come from the actual tasks and responsibilities but from the mental clutter that occupies our minds. For example, if you are at work and start to mentally run through the things that need to be done, and before you even start the day, you think about how you need to reschedule an appointment, pick up your kids from school, pay the monthly bills, drop off your car at the auto shop, and then go home to continue there. By then, you have already added to the pressure of what needs to be done by thinking of them over and over in your mind.

Another example would be a person who is nervous about giving a fifteen-minute presentation. The hours spent anticipating and worrying for days before the event happens adds to the stress level, which causes the feeling of being overwhelmed.

So, how are we supposed to handle these overwhelming situations? We start by asking ourselves some very important questions and then answering those questions honestly.

How I Got into This Mess

Diana: As I was looking back, I thought I had my year all planned out. Around mid-December, I set my goals for 2016 and laid out a plan for how I was going to accomplish my goals. I even outlined the action steps in order to achieve my financial, physical, relationship, and spiritual goals. Then I looked at what projects I had committed to and saw that even though I was taking the lead role in two of them, I had good people around me who were more than capable of doing a great job, which, in turn, would make my job easier to manage. From there, I looked at my schedule for the year and saw that I had plenty of time to prepare great things that are yet to come. I even got myself an assistant just in case I needed additional help with my workload. I entered all of that information into my smartphone and saved it as I smiled, thinking, *Life is good.*

Yet, not even two months into the New Year, I found that I already had more on my plate than I could handle. My leadership projects were spread out thinly with unexpected obstacles. Though I was working longer hours than I originally planned, deadlines were closing in on me. With all of the business that I was dealing with, which were my major projects, other important goals for my life started to fall apart. Instead of keeping a healthy diet and getting at least eight hours of sleep, I started eating foods that gave me nothing good in return and would stay up late doing my best to meet deadlines. Even my assistant was working late to complete tasks I no longer had time to do.

I asked myself, *How in the world did I get myself into this mess?* Upset with the way I was handling the situation, I came up with a plan to shake off the defeated feeling and regain control of my life. I knew that I had to snap out of the negative mode I put myself in by becoming overwhelmed. I knew that I was not doing myself any favors.

I asked myself some important questions that needed honest answers, and they are as follows:

- Did I anticipate the unforeseen?
- Have I agreed to do more than I am capable of doing?
- Are the goals that I have set for myself clearly set?
- Am I not managing my time correctly?
- Am I doing things that are the responsibility of others?
- Am I spending time on worthless things?

Asking questions like these can help us see where things started to decline. Plus, it is beneficial to ask the people around you to answer some of these questions about yourself. Once we have answered these questions, we can then overcome the awful feeling of being overpowered by our circumstances.

Succeeding the Feeling of Being Overwhelmed

Feeling like you are overwhelmed and actually being overwhelmed are basically the same thing. Some people have multiple projects that they cannot handle, while others may have one task to do that seems so large it appears overwhelming. Either way, the person maintains a feeling that causes him or her physical and mental weakness that makes the person unable to perform at his or her best.

But before we can regain control of our lives again, we have to learn to handle that overwhelming feeling. There are several ways to handle the helpless feeling of being overwhelmed. Here are the best ways I have found to combat this terrible emotion:

Once in a while, stop everything you do for the day.

The world around us is created to keep us moving forward. We have smartphones and drive-through restaurants, and everything seems to be done at a fast pace, including turbo internet connections. The marketing strategy behind all of these things is the promise that your life will be easier, and you will have more time for the important things. Even with all of these advances that are supposed to make life easier, where we are still busier than ever.

Before we can take back control of our lives, we need to stop the life we are currently living for a moment and readjust ourselves to a better lifestyle. Therefore, do not check your social media accounts, read another email, take another phone call, or do anything else until we have stopped everything to reexamine our situations.

Prayer is a form of meditation and vice versa.

Meditation is conscious relaxation and is a super effective way to increase focus in order to address the problems that are in the mind. Clarity of vision is important, regardless of what we are doing or in which direction we are headed. Sitting quietly for fifteen minutes in the morning or evening gives your mind and body time to relax and let go of tension.

Whenever you feel the overwhelming tension, close your eyes for at least five minutes, focus only on your breathing, and then clear your mind and gather your thoughts again.

Do your best to take care of your body.

You are only going to be as good as your body allows you to be. As we get busier, our sleeping and eating habits seem to be the first to decline. Fast food saves time but is unhealthy. Sleeping fewer hours gives us more time in the day to complete our projects, but without a full night's sleep, we become less effective.

When we require more work from our minds and bodies, we should provide them with the proper foods and support to perform at their best. This fuel and support should come in the form of plenty of rest and a healthy eating plan.

Make time to have fun with friends.

One of the greatest blessings in my life is a close group of friends who I can reach out to at any time just to say, "What are you doing? I am having a rough week. Can we meet at a cafe to chat a bit? My treat." Spending time with family and friends who support you can be a great stress reliever.

I do my best to keep the details of my busy week out of conversations with family and friends. These moments with your friends should be an escape from whatever is overwhelming you. Just be in that moment and let those problems and worries disappear. The most important thing at that time should be enjoying the company of your family and friends.

Exercise is the best stress reliever.

It is well known that exercise is a great stress reliever and has great health benefits. Exercise releases endorphins into your bloodstream. Endorphins are the happy chemicals that your body produces and just a few minutes of strenuous exercise daily can be enough to prevent diabetes by lowering blood sugar. Plus, when you are active, you increase the blood flow to your brain, which will increase your thinking and focus.

Regain control when feeling overwhelmed.

Now that you are feeling much better, it is time to tackle your obstacles and regain control of your life. Taking control of your life is the best gift you can give yourself to find the better life that is waiting to be discovered. Do your best to regain control of your life when life brings you feelings of being overwhelmed. Plus, regaining control of your life brings you what is needed in life because only you know what that is.

Define what is important.

Recognizing the most important things in your life makes it easier to decide how to spend your time. My friend attended a seminar where the presenter talked about defining your big rocks. At this seminar, someone was asked to come on stage and try to fill a jar with rocks of different sizes. The person would quickly find that the only way to get all of the rocks in the jar is to place the biggest rocks first. After the big rocks are in the jar, the person found ways to fit the little rocks in more easily.

Be careful that you are not spending most of your time on the little things. Find the three most important things you need to do in a day, and then do those things first, which are considered to be the big rocks. Checking email may be important, but if it is not one of the most important tasks of your day, it should be considered a little rock.

Cut the unnecessary things.

The truth is we tend to fill our time with what we think is important. Eliminate the unnecessary things in your life that take up your time and energy.

Many of the things we do in lives are urgent but not important. What are some things in your life that take up much of your time but are not very important or do not contribute much toward your well-being? Can you work on reducing or eliminating these activities? Yes, of course, you can.

Delegating to others.

If you fear giving up control, this is going to be more difficult than you think, but the most important thing you have to do is gain back control of your life.

I had a problem with this the first time I hired an assistant because I knew how I wanted every task to be done and felt I was the best person to do it. But once I learned how to delegate tasks to other people, I wondered why I waited so long to do it.

If your personal and professional life is filled with too many little rocks, then delegating those tasks might be the solution you need. If you are going back and forth with your day-to-day tasks with a personal and professional life, then you might consider getting some help.

Saying no can be a lifesaver.

One of the major mistakes I made was saying yes to almost every project I was interested in, and even some I had no interest in but said yes to take part in just for the learning experience.

After realizing what I had done, I began saying no to all new projects that came along because I knew I would not have the time to put my best effort into it. Learning to say no may be difficult to do, but it is necessary if you want to regain control of your life. Whether the request is coming from your boss, partner, child, or coworker, if you are unable to handle any more tasks or jobs, you must say no to them.

Reward yourself for your success.

So, you completed all of your big rocks. You were able to do away of all the unimportant tasks, passed some responsibilities onto others, and said no more times this week than you had before, and after that, you were able to handle an angry toddler. This is where it all pays off.

And now that you have regained control of your life, it is now time to do something for yourself as a reward for handling the obstacles. Now is your chance to finish that book you started writing or the project you did not have time for. Maybe you would enjoy going to a new restaurant or taking a walk in the park. Perhaps you just want to lie on the couch and watch a movie to enjoy living at the moment.

Go ahead, enjoy yourself and have fun. You have earned it all and more. You deserve it all.

When you feel overwhelmed with work and life, what do you do to regain control and find balance again?

Affirmation

- I keep my thoughts on positivity and allow myself to remain calm and relaxed.

PATHWAY 49

Ways to Find Your Purpose

The purpose of life is a life of purpose.

—Robert Byrne

What are you are passionate about? What makes your heart sing and smile? The things you are passionate about are leading to your purpose and give you an inner feeling of joy and contentment.
Passion is a powerful and an intense emotion. So powerful, that when used properly, it has the potential for the highest level of achievement and fulfillment. The purpose of our lives reveals itself in our passions. Life loves when we are passionate because we are in our happiest and most creative state. Passion with the right action leads to creation that exceeds our expectations.

The immeasurable power within us is gathered in our passion and craves to thrive. So, it is a wonderful thing when passion bumps with a career. Add dedication, hard work, and positive thinking to the mix, and you have success. When you love what you do, you will always do it better and have higher results because of passion.

Are you doing what you truly love to do? Could you do more of it? If you are passionate about something, but you are not doing enough of it, chances are you are not happy. The good news is nothing is forever, even if it seems that way. You can do what you love to do and earn a good living from doing it.

Ideas to Help You Find Your Purpose in Life

Uncover your fears.

Oftentimes, our purposes are hidden under loads of junk called fears. These false little dictators chase us away from our purposes and scare us into believing we would fail if we followed our passions. Fear is false evidence appearing real.

It is never real, but it sure feels real. When we let go of fears, we are free. Usually, this series of events aligns us with our passions and our purposes almost instantly.

What are some of your biggest fears? Whatever you fear, look at the opposite, and you will surely find where your success lies. Once you discover your main passion, write down actionable steps to do more of it and then go for it.

Focus on your strengths and talents.

Our culture tends to focus on our weaknesses instead of our strengths and talents. This subconscious habit starts at an early age, and unless stopped, it roots itself into our adult years and stays. Some of us realize this and work to reverse it, while others wander around living average or unhappy lives.

Instead, let us focus on our strengths and build on making them even stronger. Let us follow what we love to do instead of trying to catch up in all areas. Our passions and purposes lie in our strengths and talents.

Do you know what your special gifts and abilities are? If you do, congratulations. You are probably well on your way to living your purpose. If you have not fully realized them yet, that is okay too. Keep searching. Life is just beginning.

Reflect on your childhood dreams.

It is understood that many of our childhood passions and dreams hold clues to our future purposes, but most people do not realize that and are not encouraged at an early age to pursue them. As a result, they usually do not discover them until they are well into their adult or middle-aged years.

You cannot turn back time, but you can write down memories of things you passionately enjoyed as a child. Answer these questions to find out more:

- What were you really excited about in life?

- Where did you receive the most compliments and from whom?

- What were you good at?

Children are pure love and innocence. Children are their authentic selves. Our authentic selves can reveal our best selves.

As you answer the questions above and reflect on them, notice which area makes you feel really good right now. This is your calling.

Follow what feels right.

Your soul is your best guide. It is the connection to your Creator and access to endless, divine energy. It is who you truly are, and it is the source that guides you. Are you listening to your soul?

You will know if you are on the right path if what you are doing feels right. When something feels right and you follow it, the energy builds, and passion is created. The more you follow your passion, the more creative ideas that will flow from it. These creative ideas will lead you to your purpose.

Your purpose can be different at various times in your life, and that is a good sign. We are not meant to be here to do one thing. Our purposes can be big or small, depending on how we look at it. For example, our purpose could be following a career path, learning a new skill, being a parent, being a helpful friend, volunteering, and so on.

When we follow our passions and things truly feel right in our hearts and minds, we can always be assured we are on the right path. It is not always perfect or easy, but it is worth it.

All in all, if you are not experiencing the success you have expected in your life, you may not be putting your time and attention into what you are truly passionate about. Therefore, unlocking your purpose might take longer to achieve. Yet it can be achievable.

If you feel like you have examined all that is shared in this book and you are still not sure about your passion or purpose, try asking yourself this very simple yet profound question: *What would I be doing right now, full time, if I were guaranteed success?* The answer to that question may be your answer.

Remember, you will never fail if you follow what you love. There will be mistakes along the way, but that is how you learn and grow. The most successful and happiest people have made many mistakes along the way but, they never gave up.

If you follow your passion long enough, you will be aligned with your purpose. Consistently living that purpose will guarantee lasting fulfillment. In fact, you can bet your best life will miraculously unfold before your very eyes.

Affirmation

- What I am passionate about fills my heart with joy and excitement.

PATHWAY 50

Discovering Your Purpose

If you can't figure out your purpose, find out your passion.
For your passion will lead you right into your purpose.
—T. D. Jakes

Finding Your Purpose in Life

Believe it or not, we are all sent here for a reason, and one way or another, we all play a major role in this world. We are all born with special gifts that will contribute to a cause greater than ourselves.

A Story of My Best Friend

Diana: Not long ago my best friend was in town and stayed with me for a couple of days. As we were chatting, she told me that for the past few years, she was running full speed and going after her dream of success and money. She then told me it had slipped her mind why she was running, and luckily, that is when she came to stay with me. And as we chatted, I learned that she had achieved all the financial goals she was aiming for. She had financial independence, several successful businesses, homes in multiple countries, and the luxury to afford the finest things money could buy.

Through hard work, persistence, and dedicated action steps, she made it through just fine. Yet she was not happy. She did not have the free time to enjoy her wealthy life. She wanted a family, peace of mind, and the ability to live her life, but she was not able to. She had one too many responsibilities, too much to lose, and too many things to protect. She had spent many years building her dream, and now that it was complete, she was spending her time keeping it from falling apart.

Getting to know my best friend was a life-changing and eye-opening experience. Her words snapped me out of a state of unconsciousness. It was then that it became clear to me that I did not want to spend the rest of my life chasing after money only to find that I would be back at the same place I am today emotionally, mentally, and spiritually. My fast pace instantly came to a fast stop, everything was put on hold, and I spent the next two weeks reevaluating my life and purpose.

During the two weeks, the following questions came to mind:

- What am I going after?
- Why am I chasing it?
- What is my purpose in life?
- What is the reason I am here?

While chatting with my best friend, I told her about an article I read as to why most small businesses do not work. I told her it took me by surprise, which immediately brought tears to my heart when reading the section on finding purpose. In that section, the readers were asked to do a visualization exercise.

Through a guided meditation, you are instructed to vividly picture the day of your funeral. What do you want your eulogy to consist of?

What would your lifetime achievements be? What would matter the most at the end of your life? Is it what you are doing right now? If not, why not? What are you going to be remembered for? What would you like to be remembered for?

As I started to write, I began to list all the things that are most important to me. I wrote down all the things I wanted to do. I also reevaluated my mission statement. I decided that whatever journeys I commit to must be aligned with my mission statement, values, and goals. And when a new opportunity comes along, I will simply ask myself, "How does this align with my goals?" Regardless of how much money I could get, if my journey did not align with where I wanted to be, then I would not move forward with it.

A powerful mission statement: To empower, motivate, and inspire people to live happier, healthier, and more fruitful lives.

Some of My Values and Goals

What matters most is my connection with myself, being present, and feeling blissful. What I value most is having meaningful relationships with people and connecting with people on deep levels of the mind.

My plan is to be financially independent and to have control of my time. I plan to work only on projects and causes that I relate with. I plan to achieve my finances without damaging my values, goals, and personal mission.

I plan to travel and experience different parts of the world like I have been all my life. Experiencing different cultures, making memories, and sharing them with others is priceless.

Having my family financially secure is also important to me. I desire a deep, loving relationship with myself, my son, and all who are within my world and the ability to live every day fully, as if it were my last.

Now it is time to create your life purpose—the questions that can help you define your personal mission.

Simple Instructions

Get your journal or some paper and get ready to write. Find an area or a room where you will not be disturbed or interrupted. Turn off your smartphone, television, and computer.

Answer each question by writing down the first thing that comes to mind without editing what you write. You can use points of reference to help you out. Therefore, it is important to write out your answers instead of thinking about them.

Do your best to write your answers fast. Give yourself less than a few seconds to answer a question. If you cannot answer it fast, come back to it once you are done answering the rest. Be honest with yourself in your answers. Plus, no one will read it but you. Just keep in mind that it is important to write without editing.

Questions to Answer

What makes you smile? This includes projects, people, events, hobbies, and so on.

What were your favorite things to do in the past?

How do you spend time now?

What projects make you lose track of time and day?

What makes you feel proud about yourself?

Who inspires you the most? This can be anyone you know or do not know, such as a family member, best friend, book author, or motivational speaker.

Which qualities inspire you in each person?

What are you naturally good at, such as your skills, talent, and natural gifts?

What do people usually ask you for help with?

If you had to teach anyone something positive, what would you teach that person?

What would you regret not taking action on in life, whether it's something you have always wanted to do or something you have always wanted to be?

You are now ninety-five years of age, sitting in a rocking chair outside on your front porch. You can feel the spring wind gently brushing against your body and face. You are blissful and happy, and you are pleased with the wonderful life you have been blessed with. Looking back at your life and all that you have achieved and acquired and all the relationships you have developed, what matters to you most? List them all out one by one.

What are your deepest values? Prioritize each word in order of importance to you.

What were some challenges, difficulties, and concerns you have overcome or will be overcoming soon? How did you do it?

What purpose and/or causes do you strongly believe in? And which ones do you connect with the most?

If you could give a positive message to a large group of people attending a conference, who would those people be? What important information would your message give them?

How would you use your resources such as your talents, passions, and values to serve others in time of need, help others when they reach out to you, or contribute your part to society, including your community, causes, organizations, the environment, and Mother Earth?

There is so much that we all can do that we can all benefit from—and abundantly.

Mission Statement Is Part of Life

Write a statement that holds true to your heart and that will help you follow through with what needs to be done in order to achieve all your goals and dreams, which are your passions.

> All you have to do is write one true sentence.
> Write the truest sentence that you know.
> —Ernest Hemingway

Personal Mission Questions to Answer and Think About

- What do I want to do?
- Who do I want to help?
- What would the results be?
- What values will I create?

Creating a Personal Mission Statement

Answer the questions above as quickly as you can. List out actions words and steps that you can relate with.

For example:

- education
- achievement
- empowerment
- encouragement
- improvement
- helping
- giving
- guidance
- inspiration
- combining
- mastering
- motivating
- nurturing
- organizing
- producing
- promoting
- traveling
- sharing
- understanding
- teaching
- writing

Be creative and loving with your mission statement.

Based on your answers, list everything and everyone you believe you can help. For example: people, animals, orphanages, charities, environment, and so on. Then identify your end results to each one, which then become part of your goals. But not only that, you also need to answer how will the who, what, where, when, why, and how benefit from what you do? And what is or would be your purpose? What is or would be your mission?

Affirmation

- I seek my own purpose through a personal mission statement, stating I empower, motivate and inspire people to live a happier, healthier, and more fruitful life.

THE SILVA CENTERING EXERCISE

Explanation of the Technique

Aside from going into a nice, relaxed state of being and listening to a voice instructing a conditioning exercise, you must energize yourself, for that is how we begin our dynamic meditation.

We want you to do three basic things while you are utilizing the Silva Centering Exercise. While your eyes are closed:

First, practice concentrating. Concentration is a must, for it is the key to imagination and everything else. Just stay focused in the present moment.

Second, practice imagination. Overexaggerate. Exaggerate your imagination because you will be in a better position to control your programming. By magnifying your imagination, you will be able to better program yourself to be more effective, and it will help you keep active while going through the exercise.

You are not being encouraged to go into a hypnotic sleep, although it may happen for newcomers due to of a lack of experience with the exercise. It is normal to slip into this hypnotic state, but you will see improvement with practice. By being mentally active, you will avoid this from happening. This happens because the mind wanders off. This is another reason you should practice your concentration and practice exaggerating your imagination; this will help you remain active. These levels of mind are accomplished with conscious awareness. We must maintain our consciousness as much as we possibly can.

The third thing you must practice is to coordinate the physical relaxation with the mental relaxation.

It is easy to go into a mental relaxation. It only takes about two or three seconds once you obtain the ability to do so. In a way, you leave your body behind. This is also true for people who have taken the Silva program for four or five years. When they do the exercise, their bodies are still sitting straight up as if it is the first time they ever went through the exercise. This is an indication that they have not practiced.

Remember that we are a body-mind entity. We must relax the body and mind simultaneously. It takes a little longer for you to relax your body than it does for you to relax your mind. And in your body, there are some tissues that relax before others do. The tissues that are most sensitive relax immediately.

Entering the Alpha Level

To enter the Alpha Level, the Basic Plane Level, we normally associate and reinforce a specific number with its desired state. Therefore, we start by relating the number 6 to the outer conscious level; number 5 would be eye fatigue; number 4 eyes closed and ready to relax.

When we get to number 3, it represents Physical Relaxation. This is when you will learn how to relax completely from head to toe, taking your time. You will concentrate your attention on different parts of your body, releasing and relaxing tension and negative pressures as you go.

Number 2 represents Mental Relaxation; it is a state where you will imagine yourself in peaceful scenes.

Number 1 is the Basic Plane Level that you can learn to use for any purpose you desire. This is when the imagination takes place and when solutions are found.

True relaxation means relaxing the body and mind while slowing brain waves.

When we say *deeper*, it does not refer to brain frequencies. Instead, we use words such as *lower* and *deeper*. In fact, when you practice and reach a deeper level of mind, you have a heightened sense of awareness.

Silva Centering Exercise Technique

Deepening

Physical Relaxation at Level 3.

Find a comfortable position, close your eyes, take a deep breath, and, while exhaling, mentally repeat and visualize number 3 three times. To help you learn to relax physically at Level 3, direct your attention to different parts of your body.

Concentrate your sense of awareness on your scalp, the skin that covers your head; you will detect a fine vibration, a tingling sensation, a feeling of warmth caused by circulation. (Pause.) Now release and completely relax all tensions and ligament pressures from this part of your head and place it in a deep state of relaxation that will grow deeper as we continue.

Concentrate your sense of awareness on your forehead, the skin that covers your forehead; you will detect a fine vibration, a tingling sensation, a feeling of warmth caused by circulation. Now release and completely relax all tensions and ligament pressures from this part of your head and place it in a deep state of relaxation that will grow deeper as we continue.

Concentrate your sense of awareness on your eyelids and the tissue surrounding your eyes; you will detect a fine vibration, a tingling sensation, a feeling of warmth caused by circulation. Now release and completely relax all tensions and ligament pressures from this part of your head and place it in a deep state of relaxation that will grow deeper as we continue.

Concentrate your sense of awareness on your face, the skin covering your cheeks; you will detect a fine vibration, a tingling sensation, a feeling of warmth caused by circulation. Now release and completely relax all tensions and ligament pressures from this part of your head and place it in a deep state of relaxation that will grow deeper as we continue.

Concentrate on the outer portion of your throat, the skin covering your throat area; you will detect a fine vibration, a tingling sensation, a feeling of warmth caused by circulation. (Pause.) Now release and completely relax all tensions and ligament pressures from this part of your body and place it in a deep state of relaxation that will grow deeper as we continue.

Concentrate within the throat area and relax all tensions and ligament pressures from this part of your body and place it in a deep state of relaxation, going deeper and deeper every time.

Concentrate on your shoulders; feel your clothing in contact with your body. (Pause.) Feel the skin and the vibration of the skin covering this part of your body. Relax all tensions and ligament pressures and place your shoulders in a deep state of relaxation, going deeper and deeper every time.

Concentrate on your chest; feel your clothing in contact with this part of your body. (Pause.) Feel the skin and the vibration of your skin covering your chest. Relax all tension and ligament pressures and place your chest in a deep state of relaxation, going deeper and deeper every time.

Concentrate within the chest area; relax all organs; relax all glands; relax all tissues, including the cells themselves, and cause them to function in a rhythmic, healthy manner.

Concentrate on your abdomen; feel your clothing in contact with this part of your body. (Pause.) Feel the skin and the vibration of your skin covering your abdomen. Relax all tension and ligament pressures and place your abdomen in a deep state of relaxation, going deeper and deeper every time.

Concentrate within the abdominal area; relax all organs; relax all glands; relax all tissues, including the cells themselves, and cause them to function in a rhythmic, healthy manner.

Concentrate on your thighs; feel your clothing in contact with this part of your body. Feel the skin and the vibration of your skin covering your thighs. (Pause.) Relax all tension and ligament pressures and place your thighs in a deep state of relaxation, going deeper and deeper every time.

Sense the vibrations at the bones within the thighs; by now, these vibrations should be easily detectable.

Concentrate on your knees; feel the skin and the vibration of your skin covering the knees. (Pause.) Relax all tensions and ligament pressures and place your knees in a deep state of relaxation, going deeper and deeper every time.

Concentrate on your calves; feel the skin and the vibration of the skin covering your calves. (Pause.) Relax all tensions and ligament pressures and place these parts of your body in a deep state of relaxation, going deeper and deeper every time.

To enter a deeper, healthier level of mind, concentrate on your toes. Enter a deeper, healthier level of mind.

To enter a deeper, healthier level of mind, concentrate on the soles of your feet. Enter a deeper, healthier level of mind.

To enter a deeper, healthier level of mind, concentrate on the heels of your feet. Enter a deeper, healthier level of mind.

Now cause your feet to feel as though they do not belong to your body.

Feel your feet as though they do not belong to your body. (Pause.) Your feet feel as though they do not belong to your body.

Your feet, ankles, calves, and knees feel as though they do not belong to your body.

Your feet, ankles, calves, knees, thighs, waist, shoulders, arms, and hands feel as though they do not belong to your body.

You are now at a deeper, healthier level of mind, deeper than before.

This is your Physical Relaxation Level 3. Whenever you mentally repeat and visualize the number 3, your body will relax as completely as you are now, and more so every time you practice.

Deepening

Mental Relaxation at Level 2.

To enter the Mental Relaxation Level 2, mentally repeat and visualize the number 2 several times, and you are at Level 2, a deeper level than 3. (Pause.) Level 2 is for mental relaxation, where noises will not distract you. Instead, noises will help you to relax mentally more and more.

To help you learn to relax mentally at Level 2, place your attention to different passive scenes. Visualizing any scene that makes you tranquil and passive will help you relax mentally.

Being at the beach on a nice summer day may be a tranquil and passive scene for you.

A tranquil and passive scene for you may be a walk through the woods on a beautiful summer day when the breeze is just right, where there are tall shade trees, beautiful flowers, a very blue sky, an occasional white cloud, birds singing in the distance, even squirrels playing on the tree limbs. Hear birds singing in the distance.

This is Mental Relaxation Level 2, where noises will not distract you.

To enhance Mental Relaxation at Level 2, practice visualizing tranquil and passive scenes.

To Enter Level 1

Mentally repeat and visualize the number 1 several times.

You are now at Level 1, the Basic Plane Level where you can function from your center.

Deepening Exercises

To enter deeper, healthier levels of mind, practice with the Countdown Deepening Exercises.

To deepen, count downward from 100 to 1, 50 to 1, or from 25 to 1. When you reach the count of 1, you will have reached a deeper, healthier level of mind, deeper than before.

You will always have full control and complete dominion over your faculties and senses at all levels of the mind, including the outer conscious level.

When to Practice

The best time to practice the Countdown Deepening Exercises is in the morning when you wake up. Remain in bed at least five minutes practicing the Countdown Deepening Exercises.

The second-best time to practice is at night when you are ready to retire.

The third best time to practice is at noon after lunch.

Five minutes of practice is good. Ten minutes is very good. Fifteen minutes is excellent.

To practice once a day is good. Two times a day is very good. Three times a day is excellent.

If you have a health problem, practice for fifteen minutes three times a day.

To Come Out of Levels

To come out of any level of the mind, count to yourself mentally from 1 to 5 and tell yourself that at the count of 5 you will open your eyes, be wide awake, and feeling fine and in perfect health, feeling better than before.

Then proceed to count slowly from 1 to 2, then to 3, and at the count of 3, mentally remind yourself that at the count of 5, you will open your eyes and be wide awake, feeling fine and in perfect health, feeling better than before.

Proceed to count slowly to 4 and then to 5. At the count of 5 and with your eyes open, mentally tell yourself, "I am wide awake, feeling fine and in perfect health, feeling better than before. And this is so."

Deepening Routine Cycle

To help you enter a deeper, healthier level of mind, count back from 10 to 1. On each descending number, you will feel yourself going deeper, and you will enter a deeper, healthier level of mind.

10, 9 Feel yourself going deeper.
8, 7
6 Deeper and deeper.
5, 4
3 Deeper and deeper.
2, 1

You are now at a deeper, healthier level of mind, deeper than before.

You may enter a deeper, healthier level of mind by simply relaxing your eyelids. Relax your eyelids. (Pause.) Feel how relaxed they are. (Pause.) Allow this feeling of relaxation to flow slowly downward throughout your body, all the way down to your toes. (Pause.)

It is a wonderful feeling to be deeply relaxed—a very healthy state of being.

To help you enter a deeper, healthier level of mind, count from 1 to 3. At that moment, you will project yourself mentally to your ideal place of relaxation.

1 (pause), 2 (pause), 3. Project yourself mentally to your ideal place of relaxation. Relax. (Pause.)

Relax. (Pause.) Take a deep breath, and as you exhale, relax and go deeper. (Pause.)

Here is where you'll do your programming by working on your problems and how to solve them. The Alpha Level is where you want to take your time to analyze issues and come up with step-by-step solutions.

The Silva Centering Exercise is to correct the problem mentally. When using this technique, make sure you lock it in with the Three-Fingers Technique before coming out of Level.

The Three-Fingers Technique

While at the Alpha Level, bring together the tips of the first two fingers and thumb of either hand, your consciousness adjusts to a deeper level of awareness for stronger programming. Stronger programming of information results in easier recall, producing a better memory.

The reason is simple: The Three-Finger Technique contains all the elements of successful programming. Each finger represents a subjective energy: Desire, Belief, and Expectancy. Together, the three add up to Faith.

Imagination is essential to success; when you imagine a free parking space, your focus shifts inward, your brain frequency slows, and you go to level, causing rewards above and beyond what you can imagine.

Dream Control, Step One.

To practice remembering a dream, you will enter Alpha with the Three-to-One Method. Once at your level, you will mentally tell yourself, *I want to remember a dream, and I am going to remember a dream.* You will then go to sleep from Level 1. You will awaken during the night or in the morning with a vivid recollection of a dream. Be ready to record your dream. When you are satisfied that Dream Control step one is responding, then start with Step Two.

Dream Control, Step Two.

To practice remembering more than one dream per night, enter Alpha with the Three-to-One method. Once at Level, mentally tell yourself, *I want to remember my dreams, and I am going to remember my dreams.* You will then go to sleep from Level 1. You will awaken several times during the night and in the morning with vivid recollections of your dreams. Be ready to record your dreams. When you are satisfied that Dream Control Step Two is responding, then start with Step Three.

Dream Control, Step Three.

To practice generating a dream that you can remember, understand, and use for problem-solving, you will enter Alpha with the Three-to-One method. Once at Alpha, mentally tell yourself, *I want to have a dream that contains information to solve the problem I have in mind.* State the problem, and add, *I will have such a dream, remember it, and understand it.* You then go to sleep from Level 1. When you awaken with a recollection of the desired dream, you will record the dream and understand it. And this is so.

Bring Out

In a moment, count from 1 to 5. At that moment, you will open your eyes, be wide awake, feeling fine and in perfect health, feeling better than before. You will have no ill effects whatsoever in your head, no headache; no ill effects whatsoever in your hearing, no buzzing in your ears; no ill effects whatsoever in your vision and eyesight; vision, eyesight, and hearing improve every time you function at these levels of mind.

1, 2 Coming out slowly now.

3 At the count of 5, you will open your eyes, be wide awake, feeling fine and in perfect health, feeling better than before, feeling the way you feel when you have slept the right amount of revitalizing, refreshing, relaxing, healthy sleep.

4, 5 Eyes open, wide awake, feeling fine and in perfect health, feeling better than before.

Wide awake, feeling fine, and in perfect health. And this is so.

It is recommended that everyone practice staying at your center for fifteen minutes a day to balance the body and mind.

Diana Silva, daughter of Jose Silva – the man credited with bringing modern day meditation to the West, has lived her entire life dedicated to helping others. Diana has over 30 years of experience supporting Silva Graduates and the International Community of Silva Instructors.

Her unique approach combines the Silva Method Mental Techniques with state-of-the-art coaching methodologies to bring her clients to a more advanced way of living. She is President of Silva International, a mentor, and friend to Silva Graduates throughout the world. She has helped hundreds of people believe in themselves, use Silva to advance their lives, and overcome personal limitations.

Diana helps you live from your heart, which is your intuition and explores the consequences of not trusting this guidance. She helps you understand the tools and techniques of the Silva Method.

Diana also brings clarity to what was covered in a live event from the comfort of your own home. Diana is a good listener with a compassionate heart. Her passion is to help others by helping them find a solution to what they are eager to change. She helps find solutions by applying what you have learned from the Method and will continue to learn. She is truly an honest and non-judgmental listener. She pushes you to search your inner self while also taking the necessary steps to live the life of your dreams.

Her goal is to bring you reasonable, rational, and clear solutions that will result in daily improvements to your life.

Being part of the Silva International team for so many years has provided insight into what areas of life are most common challenges for humanity. Most of the daily challenging calls pertain to relationships, jobs, and health. Diana helps people find their true love, their soul mate, and their happiness in life by learning to love others and yourself with balance and boundaries. She also helps individuals who are looking for a job or a new career path to get in touch with their life's purpose. When it comes to personal health she helps you understand the spiritual-based steps that begin first in the real world. This integrative approach is powerful and effective.

The Silva Method is part of who she is. Diana can say that she has practiced it all her life. She meditates three times a day, or even more when she is programming for someone who is need of healing. She is a giver by nature and is always ready and willing to help. You will find her fun and loving personality to be one of the best parts of working with Diana.